WHY WE PLAY

WHY WE PLAY

HOW MILLENNIALS ARE REWRITING SPORTS MARKETING

YASMEEN SHARARA

NEW DEGREE PRESS

WHY WE PLAY

How Millennials Are Rewriting Sports Marketing

ISBN   978-1-5445-0030-0   *Paperback*

       978-1-5445-0031-7   *Ebook*

CONTENTS

ABOUT THE AUTHOR

Yasmeen is a nature girl at heart. You can always count on finding her tying on her sneakers before going on long hikes or runs. Her favorite thing to do is go out exploring. There are few things in life that make her happier than great company, places, and food.

INTRODUCTION

———

Marketing: (noun) simply defined by the Merriam Webster dictionary, it is the process or technique of promoting, selling, and distributing a product or service.

Sport: (noun) a term of endearment overly used (if we are being exact, it was used 41 times) in *The Great Gatsby* by Gatsby himself, when referring to Nick as his old friend. For instance, "having a good time old sport?" or "it's pretty, isn't it old sport?"

Sport: (noun) simply defined by the Merriam Webster dictionary, it is (1) a contest or game in which people do certain physical activities according to a specific set of rules and compete against each other, (2) a physical activity that is done for enjoyment.

Now that we have both terms broadly defined, what if we put them together?

If we are giving sports marketing a more textbook definition, Wikipedia defines it as a subdivision of marketing, which focuses both on the promotion of sports events and teams, as well as the promotion of other products and services through sporting events and sports teams.

To be honest, I really dislike that definition. I may be extremely biased when I say this, but I genuinely think sports marketing is so much more than a textbook definition or a chunk of words that you memorize to spit back out on a written exam in class. Maybe I am a geek and believe that sports marketing is the coolest thing ever. But have you ever looked at that one ad that just gave you goosebumps? I have seen so many of them. The ones that can change your life in a blink of an eye and you did not even realize it. Maybe I am so passionate about sports marketing because it is what I want to do later on. I dream of making an ad that someone can watch and it made them want to go out and go on a run, or even a walk. Something. Anything really.

I first thought about sports marketing in a course I took called Marketing Strategy and Analytics, when my professor showed us an advertisement that Gatorade made of Serena Williams. It started with her as a kid and an innocent question was asked to her: "If you were a tennis player, who would you want to be like?" The ad shows her ups and downs, with of course, powerful music playing in the background that has you, the viewer, nearly chewing your nails because you are stressed for her during her downs, but get excited for her during her ups. It ends with Serena as a kid answering: "Well, I would like people to be like me."

Mic drops.

Is there any better answer?!

THAT is sports marketing to me. It is where your emotions get involved, and you want to jump on your couch like Tom Cruise once did, or pump your fist in the air like Judd Nelson does at the end of *The Breakfast Club*, because you just KNOW you did something absolutely unbelievable.

* * *

Even though *The Great Gatsby* may be one of my favorite books of all time, that kind of term of endearment is not what I will be basing my book off of. Going off the Merriam Webster definition of the word *sport*, do you remember the first time you played your favorite sport or watched it on TV?

Your favorite sports team? Or, do you remember the first time you saw an athlete and told yourself that you wanted to be just like them when you were older?

Looking back on all these questions is a trip down memory lane. I can tell you the first time I played soccer and bruised my legs until they were entirely blue, or I can tell you the first time I picked up a tennis racket and accidentally sent a ball straight for my tennis coach's genitals (he was in pain for a while), or the first time I tried to make a flip turn in a swimming pool when learning to competitively swim. Even though I grew up in Maryland, I can tell you why my favorite soccer team is Bayern Munich, and my favorite football team is the Patriots.

There is a story for everything. My dad is fresh off the boat from Lebanon, where sports is not a thing. When he came to the U.S. in his early twenties, he chose his teams. I grew up loving those teams because he cheered them on. No rhyme? Maybe, because I grew up in Maryland. Reason? Plenty, because my dad is my hero and wanting to be just like him, I had to like the same teams as him. It was my way of hoping he would be proud of me.

I grew up swimming, playing tennis, and soccer. I can honestly say those three sports really shaped me as a person. Being an athlete is a lot more than walking around in sweaty apparel all the time, or your hair constantly up in a ponytail, or worn out sneakers. Being an athlete has made me a much more disciplined person, a more motivated person, a go-getter, better at time management, and extremely dedicated at whatever I set my mind at.

I loved tennis so much. I knew every professional players' statistics and could tell you how fast Rafael Nadal or Roger Federer could serve a ball. I wanted to play college tennis, and I knew if I put my mind to it, I could get recruited at any program I wanted. However, life does not always follow through with your plans, and I tore half my lateral meniscus junior year of high school. My plans had changed, but I hadn't as a person.

When I started college at Georgetown University, I felt so weird the first two weeks of my freshman year having so much "free time" not playing a sport. Playing a sport has always been at the essence of who I am as a person, and I felt lost. Later that first semester on my way to the library, two beautiful tall seniors on the Varsity Men's Lightweight Crew team walked up to me and said "you are tiny and short, would you want to be a coxswain on the crew team?" I was so confused but found myself on the crew team the next day. Of course I, of all people, would pick up a sport I had never done before so late in my life just to keep sports in my everyday life.

Being on the crew team was quite an adventure, being up at ungodly hours to go to practice on the Potomac, no matter the weather. My coach sent us a funny e-mail once where everything was in the subject, but no content was actually in the e-mail. The e-mail's subject was "We will always have practice no matter the weather even in the rain or snow." That basically meant that there was no excuse to ever skip practice, which instilled in me a sense of dedication to my own workouts once I did end up leaving the crew team for family reasons after a two-year stint on it.

Once I was off the crew team, I was worried I lost my identity. Who was I? What was I studying? What did I want to do after graduation? I started training for a half-marathon because I felt like I needed something to get up and work after every morning before my classes, since the crew regiment was so instilled in me. Somehow, it clicked one day that my dream job would be to go into sports marketing. After years of chasing after sports on the actual turf, field, pool, or the Potomac, I knew I had to continue to chase after sports in the classroom.

It is interesting to see how everything that happens in your life ends up shaping you in some way. I know my experiences have made me more motivated and dedicated to the sports marketing field because it is so meaningful to me.

* * *

All the boys back home are going to business school, she said, and then they all plan to become bankers. She rolled her eyes, adding: "Everyone does the same thing - so boring."

- PHIL KNIGHT, *SHOE DOG*, PAGE 67

Reading Phil Knight's memoir *Shoe Dog*, this quote resonated with me. For most college students — particularly those in a business school — there is a sort of unspoken frenzy around most students during "recruiting season." If you ask people what they want to do after graduation, you get the same type of answer from most students, *Oh you know, consulting or investment banking, something like that.* No, but what do YOU want to do. That is really my question, but I usually let it go.

But what I have realized is that is the easy answer. The answer that is obvious. The answer that is the safe one.

Much like in sports, I never gravitated to the easy answer. That's why I would hit 1000 serves a day. That's why I ran the extra miles in the summer. That's why I spent the extra hours in the weight room. That's why I never missed practice at 5 am on the Potomac.

That's what sports does. When it's your passion, it's not easy. It just is your life.

And that's why I felt the same pull towards the world of sports marketing. Any field that could make me feel close to the field, close to that emotion of the fans, and close to the way Serena Williams' answer gave me chills.

And that's the book. The story of sports marketing — told through the eyes of a young athlete who has chosen to make this her career.

No I did not choose to write this book to try to show my "superior" knowledge about the sports marketing industry - it is actually the contrary. I had two choices: (1) go through the regular career recruiting path that every other student chooses to go through, or (2) take a huge risk and dive into my passion. I'd like to consider myself really lucky because I know what I am passionate about. As a woman trying to break into the sports marketing industry, every time I have said that my dream job is to work for Nike or Under Armour, I have never failed to get an answer like: *But you are a girl, do you know how hard that is? Have you thought of something easier? What if the pay is not that good? You know girls have a tougher time breaking into that industry, right? No offense but as a girl, no one will take you seriously.*

Honestly, offense taken.

What makes me less qualified to work in an industry that I

am passionate about just because I am a woman? I decided to write a book on the sports marketing industry. Yes, a book.

I chose to write this book because I am extremely passionate about the sports industry, and absolutely love how powerful and awe-inspiring marketing can be. While reading Phil Knight's book, the previous quote really hit a home run with me. Currently, most of my friends, heck most business school students, take the safe route and go into investment banking even if that is not what they *want* to do, but just because "that is where the money is Yas." I used to get so nervous that taking the path that is less traveled on, I was doing the wrong thing.

The thing is, I would rather go into marketing than follow what everyone else is doing because they are doing what is convenient and conventional rather than taking the harder and riskier, but more rewarding path, to follow their passion.

I know someone whose father was incredibly successful in the business industry, has two older brothers that are also very successful working in investment banking firms, and that person is now going to work at a really good investment management corporation. It all sounds really glamorous in theory, but when you ask that person if they like what they are doing, their voice lacks passion. I can tell that they do not really know what they want to do, but settled for what seemed like the best option.

And here's the crazy part, if you really get the truth from someone — the honest, raw, four-hour midnight conversation — everyone is secretly just like me. They don't want the safe route; they want something that makes them so fired up they sprint down to the waterfront.

If you find a job or a career where you would rather get so many rejections and be sad for a while about those rejections but are chasing after your passion, then you owe it to yourself.

I was rejected from a rotational program I had applied to at an advertising company I thought would be nice to work for, and did not get upset for not getting the job, but got upset because I feel like I have been getting so many misses and no hits at all. I *know* I am so qualified and would be really good at whatever I do because I am a passionate individual, and as much as my parents texted me saying its "their loss" it was still not the best of feelings. Walking home that day, I realized that I would rather have that little ache in my heart from rejections because I am brave enough to take risks and chase what I am passionate about. I am putting myself out there, and I know I am getting closer to having that home run that makes everything worth it. I can't wait to find out what that will be, but until then, I'm just enjoying the ride, even all the bumps that come along with it.

This book is because I want another woman, another girl, to

believe in her dream of breaking into the sports marketing industry. Sports and sports marketing are incredible fields and has been incredibly shaped and influenced by millennials. And it's not a man's world, or an experienced person's world... frankly it's our world.

Extremely influential, yet still incredibly young, the millennial has shaped multiple industries in a rather quick timeframe. Whether we realize it or not, millennials are at the backbone of what has come to be seen as a change in the way sports marketing is not only perceived, but the way sports marketing has to be done in order for it to be effective at targeting and acquiring customers. As you'll read in the first chapter, the millennials I spoke with have incredible insights on what companies are dealing with nowadays when it comes to sports marketing. Sports marketing has evolved so much since it first started because sports has become not only a sort of outlet for the millennial but also has a deeper significance.

✶ ✶ ✶

If you remember sports as important milestones in your life, you also probably remember to some extent what you were wearing, or if not the exact outfit, the brand. And if that is true, you probably have stayed loyal to that brand, or not strayed too far when purchasing other brands or products.

Same goes for watching ads when you are watching your favorite sports on TV. No matter how much a person can say they don't watch sports, they have at least followed the Olympics or the World Cup once every four years. When watching those events, even the least athletic of consumer becomes subject to unintentionally being influenced by the brand the athletes or Olympians are wearing. That is the subtlest form of sports marketing, but remains a form of sports marketing nonetheless, and a strategic one at that.

As sports have changed, so has its marketing and its consumer as well. The origin of sports marketing in the United States can be traced all the way back to baseball with Tops Bubble Gum and the baseball cards that came with it. This book will go back and trace the History of sports marketing, as well as how it has changed over the years, or what practices have remained the same but have been adapted to our present day. There are multiple forms of sports marketing that exist, and this book will go into detail on what kind of strategies companies use, and what companies seem to dominate the industry as well.

Not only that, but this book will touch upon the various methods of sports marketing, as well as look at the greatest campaigns that have come out of those companies and brands that most consumers would have never associated with sports marketing. They were extremely effective, since consumers associate the ads with the brand and not the sport.

This book is for the crazy ones like me; the people who love sports and love how marketers tap into that passion to bring us to their products and their communities. And as a young millennial woman, I am all in.

In the words of Serena:

"Well, I would like people to be like me."

Come along for the ride with me.

PART 1

ORIGINS OF SPORTS MARKETING

CHAPTER 1

STORYTELLERS: HOW MILLENNIALS & MILLENNIAL ATHLETES ARE REWRITING THEIR STORIES

"I like the challenge of getting players to rise to certain levels, but that's the easy part. The biggest challenge is to get them to believe in what we're doing. They have to understand that it's O.K. to have good days and bad days."

- TEMPLE WOMEN'S BASKETBALL COACH AND
FORMER WNBA PLAYER, DAWN STALEY

* * *

"Durant seeks a ring through opportunity, rather than accomplishment. Turns out Durant was ready to leave OKC, the franchise and the place, and was a typical Millennial," wrote a clearly biased and agitated Berry Tramel of The Oklahoman.

"I know back in the day, I couldn't imagine going to the Lakers and playing with Magic Johnson." Larry Bird offered his take on Durant.

"Don't give a damn what anyone says: weak move by KD," Stephen A. Smith wrote on Twitter. "You go to GSW, the team who beat you, when you're already on a title contender? Please!"

Kevin Durant quietly and respectfully leaves the team that drafted him, that he'd brought to the NBA championships and that had earned him millions. And he's a typical Millennial? Exercising his opportunities and choices; going to the place he could win a championship; optimizing his flexibility.

Wow...

* * *

KD and I have one thing in common: we are both part of the Millennial Generation (born between 1982 and 2004).

And as it turns out the media loves to hate us. Whether it's twenty-somethings like Bryce Harper who wants to make baseball fun again or LeBron James unafraid to come up with elaborate handshakes and poses for each teammate before games or Odell Beckham unafraid to pay fine after fine for celebrating (and sometimes proposing to the kicking net).

Anna Liotta, the author of "Unlocking Generational Codes" offers a unique take on the Millennial generation. Liotta writes about the impact of September 11, 2001 on Millennials. Most of us were youngsters on the day we saw our country attacked and the Twin Towers brought down by terrorists. Liotta says Millennials were significantly affected by the images and violence, and what transpired afterwards. She says that in that day, suddenly, the world seemed much less safe.

"One of the key things that 9/11 left with (Millennials) is urgency and immediacy," Liotta said. "So where prior generations would have said, be a millionaire by the time you're 40, our Millennials, without really articulating it, (indicate) that things need to speed up. — I need to do things sooner, faster. I need to accomplish, because I don't know that the world is here tomorrow."

"You hear a lot of people saying Millennials walk in on Day 1 and by Day 30 they expect to run the joint. What happened? Why can't they wait their turn? Why don't they do their time in the trenches? That's how that shows up in success, is this immediacy of, 'Hurry up, hurry up, hurry up, I'm not patient, I'm not going to wait my turn.'?"

And that's what KD and I share in common:

No. We won't wait our turns.

* * *

Millennial athletes are not our parent's sports heroes.

And the millennials who buy jerseys from stars like Harper, come early to watch shooting drills with James, or buy products endorsed by Beckham, see the world through a different lens.

We are storytellers. And whether we are fans or we are thinking about how our brands can engage those fans, we are thinking differently.

Millennials are the newest, largest and fastest growing segment of customers brands are now courting. And we (millennials) are no longer looking for just the quality of the product; we are looking for the inspiration, for something to motivate them, to get them out the door and go be the best version of themselves.

We are looking for a story we can aspire to; a person we can dream with.

Cheesy? Absolutely! The thing is, the millennial is so much more emotional and needs something to target their emotions because an effective inspirational is more likely to speak to them and connect with them.

There is a sense of individuality when it comes to each athlete.

To understand how sports marketing has evolved to address today's largest demographic base — and it's current crop of millennials stars — I talked to dozens of millennials to understand their love of sports, the heroes they worship and how they see sports and sports figures as powerful ambassadors for brands.

They help offer insights into some of the common questions people in sports and sports marketing wonder about the newest and largest fan base:

- Do Millennials see themselves as athletes?
- Are Millennials turning away from professional sports?
- Do Millennials love their stars the way prior generations did?
- How do sports teams and sports marketing connect with Millennials?

Hard-hitting questions... Let's get right to it then.

* * *

Sports do not build character. They reveal it.

- JOHN WOODEN

I was fortunate (at least for my first two years of college) to be an athlete (listen, being the coxswain on a boat is athletic, don't get any other ideas!) It also brought me inside the college athlete lingo. The non-athletes were known as:

NARPS (NON-ATHLETIC REGULAR PERSON)

No disrespect, but when a collegiate athlete sees a NARP wearing *our* athletic gear, we were a bit smug about it. In Harry Potter terms, NARPs are the muggles. They can't understand being an athlete... not *really*.

Then two years into my collegiate career, I left the land of being an athlete into being a NARP. And yet, nothing really changed. Sure I no longer could call myself a collegiate athlete, but I still saw myself as an athlete. I still dressed in workout clothing. I still went on runs. I still trained at the gym. And I still bounced between my athlete and NARP friends.

What really *is* an athlete then?

Bill Bowerman, famous Oregon Track and Field coach and one of the cofounders of Nike, once said, "If you have a body, you're an athlete."

On a college campus, in urban centers where millennials live and work at bars and restaurants we frequent on the weekends, it's nearly impossible to pick out who is a college athlete and who isn't. And yet talk to most millennials and many of them still see themselves as an athlete. No, they don't get the sponsored gear and no they don't get training table meals. But they would call themselves an athlete.

On a campus, many of the most athletic students you'll meet don't pick up a stick, ball or baton for their University. They pick it up for themselves. And many of those "NARPs" (myself included) have unique ways they are athletes in their own rights. Some choose to focus on their education instead of playing a sport in college. Others prefer to leave the demands and structure of athletics to their high school years and no longer pursue "competitive" sports because they don't have that time.

But most of them still find a way to make it a priority, putting in the time and effort to play that sport "casually", going on their daily run, being at the gym nightly or play on a club team.

Yes, they are athletes even without the "letterman's jacket".

I wanted to understand how Millennial athletes see sports, athletes and the products that connect us to the sports and sports stars. Because the definition of being an athlete has truly expanded opening a gigantic opportunity for brands.

You'll hear stories of Rodney Williams, Declan Kelly and yes, yours truly, to understand why sports matter and how our stars inspire us.

* * *

RODNEY WILLIAMS, 21

What makes you an athlete?

"It's when you put yourself out there and play the game."

Rodney is one of the wittiest people around. From Orange County, Florida, Rodney has always been involved in sports, he started out playing tee-ball and went on to mastering volleyball, basketball, soccer, and track in middle school. He got into volleyball because his sister was "super into volleyball" and took him to a lot of intramural games every morning. Turns out, sports are contagious.

"Competing with your friends is an awesome feeling. You get to feel like you are working towards something together, which is incredible. Sometimes, you are in a rough spot and the only person you have to turn to is someone you have been best friends with since the 2nd grade. That is something indescribable."

Even as a student with a full workload, Rodney still competes 'casually' on the college's club team. He explained why he can't stop being an athlete even with the busy life of a student: "With all the work you have to do at Georgetown, I found that I always had pent up energy, and club sports helped me relieve that. It was an area I felt very comfortable in and did not want to lose that comfort."

Today Rodney religiously follows the NBA, college basketball, the NFL, and college football. But he first fell in love with hoops early in his life. Rodney said, "the first basketball game I ever got to go to was in 2002 at the Staples Center. It was the Lakers vs. the Kings. Seeing Shaq and Kobe doing their thing was unreal. When the Lakers destroyed the Kings, it was love at first sight." And it's no surprise that Kobe is and was his favorite player, "because he is so public about how driven he is to be the best. He is also one of the most clutch players of all time and shows through his game that he is always someone his teammates can depend on. I want to be someone people can depend on in pressure situations, that is why I admire Kobe. I do acknowledge that he has a pretty bad history, but I still respect his drive."

As you reflect on Rodney's words and his passion as an athlete himself for professionals like Kobe, it is as if his words come out of a Nike ad.

"When a player hits a shot and does something, I consider it as their brand being displayed. I like seeing that and thinking of ways that I can differentiate myself from every other person. Sports is a way that people can do that." Rodney loves the NBA because the players' personalities are very on display, and he is very much a personality type.

Millennials like Rodney view themselves as athletes — much in the way Bill Bowerman described all of us with a body as an athlete. Being an athlete is not only when you are physically playing a sport, but also an athlete in the classroom, an athlete in your everyday life. And that's why brands of athletic apparel are worn into class, shopping and out at night. Millennials view themselves as athletes no matter the situation.

* * *

DECLAN KELLY, 21

A process through which I can hear my own heart speak.

Besides being my secret crush from my sophomore year of college, Declan Kelly helped offer insights into why sports and sports figures remain so powerful to millennials. Declan's dad is a "sports Phenom" – having played college football and baseball, a state record holder in New York for touchdowns in high school, and drafted by the Red Sox.

"I look up to Derek Jeter because he is the hometown hero for the Yanks. He is really graceful under pressure, which is a necessary quality in life, he can tune it all out. Being stoic in life like that can help you come up in the clutch - like in an exam."

Sports are part of his first memories – mini baseball, basketball, mini hockey – "actually my dad said I had the best slap shot he ever saw, but once he put me in skates, my dad saw that I was not the most graceful skater, so ice hockey was definitely out the window." He laughed then said, "I am my dad's sports successor, an even better version, Pete 2.0."

But for Declan, sports is more than just the family tradition.

It's his place to find serenity. He wrote:

There's a lot of noise in life. A lot of noise that can get louder, angrier, and more confusing than any crowd, coach, or opponent ever could. Noise comes from everywhere. Noise is shallow. Silence is deep. That is why I'm so thankful sports gave me a path to serenity. They've given me a process through which I can hear my own heart speak. Heart, head, home, mom, dad, Con. for me, it's just that simple.

Sports gave me a greater appreciation for my family than maybe anything else. Every time I used to step up to the plate in a big game or jumped into a pool before a big race, whether a big crowd was heckling me or cheering me on, whether an opponent was screaming in my ear or a coach was whispering words of wisdom, I always thought back to my family – I'd hear my mom say three words: heart, head, home. I'd see images in my mind's eye of my dad teaching me step by step how to swing a bat when I could barely walk. I'd feel the sting in my hand from ball after ball that my brother used to throw into my mitt or the pelting of the water from his splashing in the lane next to me in kiddie league. That's why every time I stepped into the box or into the pool, I'd make the sign of the cross and tap my head three times – but it wasn't for the father the son and the holy spirit, it was for my mom, my dad, my brother, and me, with one tap for each of them, and everything would go quiet. People always used to crack jokes about my ritual. Some thought it was about God, some thought it was about me, some thought it was just plain weird, but all I knew and needed to know that was as soon as the third tap came, I could hear nothing but my own heart beating. Heart, head, home, and I would be as calm as ever.

Sports has a different meaning for everyone. For Declan, it is something that has not only given him serenity, but also "given me a process through which I can hear my own heart speak."

"Growing up, I was always known as a baseball player and a swimmer. I hold local records at the pool where I swam. I had a much tougher time letting go of swimming at the end."

Much like Rodney, another Millennial who considers himself an athlete even though he's left behind the days of competitive sports, Declan hasn't lost the love of sport and of the unique emotions it brings. "All it takes to be an athlete is a type of fearlessness, not fearlessness… That's not the right way to put it. Its the ability to rise above fear. Whether you are getting ready to walk out onto the court for a pickup basketball game, try out for a team, or make a big play in a game, you have to rise above that very human, very real, fear. The goosebumps can take ahold of you unless you can keep them still and focus. That's all it takes."

* * *

YASMEEN SHARARA, 21

Running towards things

I played tennis, volleyball, and swam throughout middle

school and high school. In college, a happy accident of being small and bumping into the crew team led me to a two year stint on the Men's Lightweight Crew Team in college.

And then I too left competitive athletics. But I didn't leave being an athlete.

I loved being a *former* collegiate athlete — a NARP. It gave me the freedom to spend my weekends studying as much as I wanted to, instead of being on a bus to our next regatta. I no longer had to wake up in the morning in a frantic to run to practice in an obscene amount of layers, just to make sure I wasn't freezing in the morning practices on the water.

I was also able to workout because I *wanted* to and not because I *had* to. After training for, and running, my first half marathon, I was hooked. I loved chasing after something that was physically and mentally challenging.

A couple months after my first half-marathon, I really could not explain what got over me, but I logged onto my computer and signed myself up for my first Olympic Distance Triathlon. I think what people forget is that when signing up for events like these, it isn't because of a goal like weight loss or to post a picture on Instagram to show your friends you did something. Maybe for some that is the case, but for me, it was to challenge myself, to work towards something and prove to myself that I am stronger than I think I am. I am not the most confident of people. I have had my fair share of things to work through in life.

I think somewhere deep down, I signed up for these things to give me an excuse to forget about what hurt me, or maybe to create a distraction.

Running my second half-marathon, a man in Under Armour leggings kept about the same pace as me the entire race. One mile he would be ahead of me; the next mile I would be ahead of him. When I was passing him at mile 12, he took out one of his earphones and said to me while smiling, "I have followed you this entire time and I am so impressed with you. Run as fast as you can this last mile. I'll see you after I cross the finish line."

I smiled realizing through sports I was never on my own; we never are. Sports represents a supportive community whether we are running, watching, attending or playing. People who understood that maybe I was running away from something, or running towards something too. He didn't need to know my story, but in that moment, he was not judging me for my past, present, or future. He was a friend.

My story around sports keeps growing and changing. And sport changes with me.

I run, I watch, I attend and I play.

And so do 54 million others like me. We don't all know what life has in store for us, but we won't wait our turns and we will continue to be athletes.

I want to run towards things.

* * *

Millennials aren't "running from sports" as some experts in the media have noted. I'd argue that more than ever we see ourselves as athletes even if we aren't playing competitively. We are embracing sports in our own ways as players, participants, fans and experiencers. As I talked to other millennials we still watch sports, but we watch differently — perhaps focusing on a player we admire or catching highlights on our phone or going for a run instead. We still embrace our sports heroes, the products they support, and their missions: but we see ourselves in them more than anything.

Millennials are emotional. We think with our hearts rather than with our brains. There is nothing wrong with that, except that most times, our parents and others question our decisions.

Maybe it's fair if you think about it. Our parents have had the same jobs for as long as they can remember. Millennials are different. We are indecisive. We are impulsive. We like to think we are spontaneous. *Go with the flow!* As some of my friends like to say.

We don't stick to one job. During recruiting season, every time I told someone I wanted to like my first job and actually enjoy what I was doing, everyone told me, "that's not how it works. You have to get a couple boring jobs before you find the one you like. You aren't going to stick to your first job. You are most likely going to be there for 2-3 years." *What? I don't want that though. Why are you telling me that is how it HAS to be??*

Millennials are like that. We like to act confident even though we sometimes have absolutely no idea what we are saying. As millennials, we are a shifty group of individuals and this has been echoed by athletes in the sports industry. And maybe in the way we consume and engage with sports and brands associated with sports.

Much like young graduates when it comes to the job search, millennial athletes choose to join teams with great names because it is the easier route, instead of making a name for themselves by standing out on a team they would rather be on. Is it wrong? Who knows. But its part of our calling to 'not wait our turns.'

Most millennials would rather get something through an opportunity than their set of skills and qualities. In all honesty, we tend to focus on the results and not the process.

I want to work hard for what I get though... Am I the odd one out?? I'd really like to hope not...

* * *

TAKEAWAY: MILLENNIALS EMBRACE SPORTS THEIR WAY

Every millennial has a story, everyone started somewhere. And with technology we are telling ours and reading our peer's stories every day. We just have different stories, we all started in a different place. We have different experiences, but at the end of the day, we are all one family, one community, and sports brings so many people together - whether it is sitting together watching the SuperBowl, running onto a field together before a lacrosse game, stretching before getting on the diving block before a swim meet, the next batter is due to bat, no one is alone.

To reach this next wave of fans, consumers and athletes will require brands, sports organizations and the players themselves to think differently. And maybe it begins with the millennial athletes we admire:

- the Durants,
- the LeBrons,
- the Harpers,
- the Beckhams,
- the Rodney/Declan/Yasmeen.

Millennials like to believe they are athletes.

The definition of what an athlete is has changed so much over time that anyone who believes they are an athlete, is one.

An athlete is somebody with a body. An athlete is putting yourself out there. An athlete is someone who doesn't give up when the going gets tough. There are endless ways to define what an athlete is, and that is because of millennials.

We don't take no for an answer, and we will not be told we are not athletes if we believe otherwise.

To millennials: everyone is an athlete.

We don't have the same definition of "athlete" as our parents do. This new perception of what an athlete is one of the reasons that millennials turn away but also run towards professional sports.

We have more means and resources to get to where we need to be, to become an Olympian. The problem is, we are no longer the only one in that boat. The appeal of dedicating your entire life to one sport, to not qualify, deters millennials.

We don't take no for an answer and we don't take rejection well.

Millennials are emotional.

We are so emotional, we feel emotional connections with the athletes we not only love, but idolize. Our parents don't get it. They had a favorite athlete they enjoyed watching on TV, but millennials took this concept up a couple notches. We put our favorite athletes on pedestals, and try everything to emulate their behavior, even by attempting to dress similarly to them.

Sports teams and sports marketing has seen this shift in fans' behaviors. Instead of communicating through posters, they have joined us on social media. For instance, Twitter updates from our favorite athletes, like this one from Michael Phelps, saying how he "Can't wait to check out the new @UAS modern American sportswear line. The line launches today and looks awesome! #BeyondAmbitious" make us feel closer than ever to our idols all while they promote a brand that sponsors them.

CHAPTER 2

TOM BRADY: THE STORY OF PICK #199

Tom Brady.

You either love him or you hate him.

As my friend Chris DeAngelo told me, "everyone in New England loves him, but others hate him because he is too successful. You hate what always beats you. It's just natural."

You hate what always beats you.

Born in 1977, Tom Brady is not only seen as the millennial's athlete, but he redefined what an athlete means. Tom Brady is not built the way the stereotypical athlete, specifically a football player, is built.

From his build, to his competitors, he had everything going against him when he was getting drafted. That is, everything, except for his belief in himself.

As draft pick #199 in the 6th round, Tom Brady was selected as a compensatory pick for the New England Patriots. He started the season as the fourth string quarterback, behind starter Drew Bledsoe, and backups John Friesz and Michael Bishop.

A lot of people don't believe in you. Its obvious by now, six other quarterbacks taken and 198 other picks. And I always thought, 'You know what? Once I get my shot, I'm gonna be ready. I'm gonna really take advantage of that.'

Tom Brady did more than just "take advantage of that." He proved to everyone that once doubted him just how wrong they were about him.

During his first season, the Patriots opened with a 23-17 loss at Cincinnati, with Bledsoe as the starting QB. During their second game, and home opener, against the New York Jets, Bledsoe suffered from internal bleeding after a hit from Jets linebacker Mo Lewis. When Bledsoe tried to return to the game, he was replaced by Tom Brady for the final series of the game. Brady came on to the field, never to come off again.

Tom Brady is not an athlete by success - he worked extremely hard to get to where he is today. An article by *Feeling Success* on Tom Brady, stated that he always remains calm under pressure, knowing that what happens during the game means nothing, and everything can turn around with a strong vision for the finish. His work ethic and ability to keep growing and learning is what makes him a winner. And it is apparent on the field or in any interview. Brady once stated "A lot of times I find that people who are blessed with the most talent don't ever develop that attitude, and the ones who aren't blessed in that way are the most competitive and have the biggest heart."

Knowing his key strengths and weaknesses are what put him on the field as the starting QB. Brady knows that football relies on more than simply the physical aspect, but it is also a sport of skill and strategy. What differentiated him from every other QB was that he knew where to be on the field, and when. Always one step ahead of everyone else.

I'm not a person who defends myself very often. I kind of let my actions speak for me. I guess in a sense I've always had a chip on my shoulder. If you were the 199th pick, you were the 199th pick for a reason: because someone didn't think you were good enough.

Being passionate about football helped keep him motivated to stay confident in the potential he had to be the great player he is today. He knew he was better than "good enough."

Tom Brady changed and redefined the boundaries of the definition the word "athlete" once had. He showed us that with hard work, anyone can be an athlete, not only the naturally talented ones. He made an athlete someone who goes out there and puts his best foot forward. Someone who is approachable, and full of personality. Someone who is both loved and hated by the general public.

My friend Chris is Tom Brady's biggest fan. I hope one day someone talks about me the way Chris talks about Tom Brady.

When I asked Chris why he liked Tom Brady, he said, "He is so handsome. Arguably the most handsome guy in the NFL. He is a family man. He always posts photos on Facebook with his kids. He also takes pay cuts to bring better people in. When Remy Moss came, he took a paycut to make sure that Moss stayed another season. Wes Welker was a nobody, but Tom Brady took a paycut to have him come onto the team. He knows better than to be selfish because he cares about his team and wants the team to be better. He always puts the team first. Aaron Hernandez, who was convicted for murder, wrote a letter talking about old players that he hated and liked in the NFL, and in that letter he said 'The closest [teammate] I was with was probably Brady in whom I love to death and always will and only hope the best for them.' That's how you know he is genuinely a really good person."

Chris knows that Tom Brady is not athletic, but he loves him for more than what he does on the field. Brady has a personality that attracts millennials.

But then again, Chris is a millennial, just like me.

I wanted to ask someone who would have wiser and more experienced insights on Tom Brady and thought of a teaching professor I got really lucky to have, Michael O'Leary.

O'Leary had incredible insights on Brady because he had a different perspective than I, or Chris would have, as millennials. He said, "As for Brady, and Coach B for that matter, I'd say they're fantastic examples of people who've figured out how to take fairly undervalued players (Brady was one himself) and fit them into a system, while also being able to adjust that system somewhat over time. I think they've also generally avoided a major star system there and have been pretty successful at giving guys second chances and having it turn out well."

Typed out in black and white, O'Leary wrote what many millennials tend to forget: *giving guys second chances and having it turn out well.*

In the sports industry, everyone tends to get so wrapped up in natural talent and ability. They forget that *practice makes perfect* is not only a cliché saying our parents used to tell us so that we wouldn't quit going to tennis practice because our arms hurt from serving so many times, but is true in the rare cases it has presented itself. Brady's being one of them.

Tom Brady is our generation's athlete.

He is loved by many because of his social media presence. He interacts with his fans on Facebook through incredibly funny and relatable posts. He recently got an Instagram, and people went crazy because the man who is seen as the G.O.A.T (greatest of all time) is closer to talking to us, than any athlete with his status was 10-15 years before. Brady values the relationships he holds with his teammates. As millennials, we are suckers for that kind of stuff.

As millennials, Brady gives us hope. He never gave up, and even walked straight up to the Patriots owner Robert Kraft and said, "I'm the best decision this organization has ever made."

Brady's unwavering confidence in himself is what attracts so many people to him. Whether people love him or hate him, Brady is the millennial's athlete.

O'Leary sent me an article that was featured in the Washington Post titled, *For Tom Brady, age is just one more remarkable number*. Tom Brady defied all odds - he somehow continually shatters people's expectations by getting better with time. One would think the older he gets, the weaker he gets. Not Tom Brady.

Do you want to know why?

The article says it is that Brady's obsession with fitness, healthy eating, and meticulous preparation is well documented. He missed all but the first game of the 2008 season with a shredded left knee. Other than that, he has made each of his 266 scheduled starts, including the playoffs, since he took over in 2001. He spoke after the Patriots completed a 14-2 regular season of the "prioritization" he places on balancing practice time and recovery.

He is a millennial athlete after all. Health and recovery is at the center of our training mentalities.

Brady practices what he preaches. Recovery is so important to him that he took it upon himself to change the way an athlete's recovery can be at night.

According to Sports Illustrated, the idea for the recovery sleep-wear came from Brady himself after he injured his calf in the 2014 season, and challenged Under Armour to incorporate it into their products. This recently released line is now known as the *TB12* line.

As the first quarterback in NFL history to have 5 Super Bowl wins, 11 Super Bowl records, and being a 4-time Super Bowl MVP in NFL history, Brady really is *the* best decision the New England Patriots ever made. When talking about Brady's history Super Bowl LI win, SB Nation wrote, "the quarterback, like a fine wine, seems to get better with age. It's hard to tell whether Brady will ever show signs of age, let alone call it quits."

Brady continually redefines what is physically possible. One of Tom Brady's teammates, Rob Gronkowski said, "I'm around Tom Brady all the time and he talks about playing forever. How can I retire before Brady?"

How can anyone retire before Brady? It would honestly be a little embarrassing if we can't do what he shows us is somehow possible.

Somehow.

The Super Bowl LI may be seen as Brady's all-time crowning achievement. This game completely redefined sports, just like Brady continuously redefines what an athlete is.

A historic game, to say the least. It was not only the biggest deficit to come back to ever in a Super Bowl game, but the first Super Bowl game ever to go into overtime.

Up until half time, you could see the Patriots, especially Tom Brady, were really nervous - his passes didn't seem to connect or have any rhyme or reason to them. The Falcons' defense was really good and was starting to make it seem like the Patriots were not going to have a shot at winning at all.

I was really nervous throughout the entire game because I came in rooting for the Patriots - wearing my Barstool shirt that had Tom Brady's drafting picture on it. I had so much faith that they would have an incredible game, but somehow the screen in front of me was showing me otherwise. At half time, everyone was making it seem like this game was over and the Patriots did not have a chance. I kept telling my dad that I had so much faith for some reason. I couldn't tell him why but I really believed they could make a come back. My best friend, Maria, was texting me saying that the Falcons deserved to win because they were the underdogs, but with a score 28-3, I couldn't understand how anyone but the Patriots could be the underdog here.

Bill Belichick was nervous. My dad was nervous. I was nervous.

After halftime, it was as if Tom Brady got his groove back and the Patriots started changing the entire course of the game. I was screaming. I was not sitting in my seat. I was standing every two minutes. I was the only girl in a room with 4 other guys, and I was louder than all of them combined. Someone told me, "I don't know what Bill Belichick does at halftime but it works every single time. The Patriots just came back and made it their game."

Their comeback was historic. Tom Brady's genius and strategies were unreal.

In an SB article about Brady's genius, Danny Amendola, who caught the 2-point conversion that tied the score in regulation, said that the win was Brady's crowning achievement. "He was the same as he always is: cool, calm and collected. He's the leader, the general, the best ever and that is the end of the story."

He is the best ever. Millennials LOVE a good story, and this game was a damn good story.

After the game, I e-mailed O'Leary and think he pegged the game better than I could, he said "it was crazy. We played horribly for three quarters, but they pulled a rabbit out of the hat at the end!" Somehow, millennials seem to find magic in everything they do.

I told my dad that I felt like the Patriots' in the Super Bowl LI was somehow my life in a game. The first half represented all the losses I have gone through, but just like Brady, I always get back up after I am sacked.

Not giving up makes it all worth it in the end.

TAKEAWAY: TOM BRADY CHANGED
THE DEFINITION OF AN ATHLETE

- As millennials, we love an underdog's story and Tom Brady's is exactly that. His success story is so compelling to us that even if we don't love him, we still talk enough about him where the saying, *no publicity is bad publicity* can be applied to him.

- Brady chose to prove himself instead of giving up on his dreams. He is at the heart of what a millennial wants to do, but he is one of the rare people to have gone out and done it - which makes him more likable to us.

- Through incredible skill and expertise, Brady has gone to show that hard work gets you what you want, even if you have to wait for your moment in the spotlight. Millennials are impatient, we want everything to happen overnight, but Brady shows us that, just like all of Michael Phelps' gold medals did not happen in a blink of an eye, his hard work eventually paid off.

- ◆ We need to be more patient
- Recovery is a new aspect of the sports industry that has not been emphasized on enough, and Brady took it upon himself to revolutionize the way an athlete recovers.
  - ◆ He makes it possible for anyone to be an athlete by being able to purchase the recovery sleepwear and not making it exclusive to only athletes of professional degrees

CHAPTER 3

EMERGENCE OF SPORTS MARKETING THROUGH BASEBALL

In chapter 1, Declan shared his story about Derek Jeter — the athlete he admired for his cool and as his hometown hero.

Baseball has played a special place for many of us, but just how American is baseball and why does it hold such a special place in the sports and sports marketing pantheon? I decided to look more into baseball and its history. Baseball is that American, homegrown sport. It is one of the first sports where people found themselves idolizing an athlete, where an athlete's status was used to influence people.

What I found out was fascinating:

If I was going to truly understand the history of marketing and sports to understand the next wave of marketing to millennials, I had to understand baseball.

* * *

"I believe baseball cards have magical powers.

"That is why, in the summer of 1988, I arranged my Dodgers cards like players on a baseball diamond on the floor of my friend Michael's Berkeley apartment. And I challenged him to do the same with his beloved Giants cards. Just moments before our teams faced off on TV, we would set them out — starters on the hardwood field, reserves side-by-side in an imaginary dugout — and sit cross-legged beside them. (And I should say at this point, we were grown men at the time; me in my 20s, Michael in his 30s.)

The cards were voodoo warriors to us, every bit as bad-ass as Chewbacca's holographic chess players. We knew, laid out on the floor, with their energy unleashed and with each of us passing his hands over them like some proud Ouija wizard, that they could make a difference, make all the difference, in the outcome of the game."

* * *

"Mom, can we please stop? A new set of rookie cards just came out this week and we haven't seen them yet. Puh-leaaaassseee!"

Growing up, I hung out more with the guys than the girls. I loved playing soccer with them, but my mom hated when I would come home with mud all over my pants, rocks in my pockets, and bruises all over my body. I used to ride to and from birthday parties with my best guy friends, and this was a frequent request I heard them ask their moms all too often, as we all sat wedged into the backseat. I didn't fully understand their infatuation with baseball cards, probably in the same way they didn't understand their friend's love of dolls, Disney princesses and Judy Moody books. It's okay, the companies behind baseball cards had mastered the appeal to their audience:

Boys.

They would receive magazines to their houses detailing the prices, the popularity and the new baseball card sets coming out in the coming months. Their moms would periodically relent and make frequent stops at our local collectibles shop, Anglo-Dutch Pools and Toys. The shop was on the way home from school and I got really good at entertaining myself while my friends would go inside and bother the store's proprietor. Yes, they'd periodically talk about NFL, NBA or NHL cards, but the real magic for my best friends was in baseball cards. As a girl, I still can't say I totally understand or appreciate their love of sports cards often saying, "Why don't you just watch them on TV?"

"Go play with your dolls," they'd jeer at me.

And they were right, I didn't get it. Turned out my best friends were the perfect target audience for the magic of baseball cards:

Sure, they loved baseball, but they *truly* loved collecting these cards.

✶ ✶ ✶

The only thing I can do is play baseball. I have to play ball. It's the only thing I know.

- MICKEY MANTLE

It turns out, my experience growing up wasn't unusual. Ask

most men about baseball cards and they'll light up — detailing their infatuation with a player, a brand and usually talking about the value of some unique, rare or one-of-a-kind card. For older individuals, the nostalgia of players and valuable cards like Mickey Mantle are evident. While younger men describe cards with a similar passion often speaking of buying and selling cards on eBay or Craigslist. But whatever the backstory, baseball cards (and the overall sports collectibles industry) is truly big business. Sports collectibles is actually a multi-billion-dollar industry.

And in many ways, the entire sports marketing industry owes its start to those small 2½ inches by 3½ inches of cardboard.

If you start researching the history of sports marketing to see where it started, how it started, and how it has changed over the years, you'll be pretty disappointed. There's really nothing tangible online to work off. Nothing at all. *How was that possible?* I tried everything to find the first documented sign of sports marketing. Again, nothing.

I figured maybe I was doing something wrong or looking for the wrong topic, so I e-mailed a couple of my old Georgetown marketing professors to ask them about their thoughts on sports marketing. They most likely would not only have knowledge on it, but some would also probably have first-hand experience. Luckily Charles Skuba got back to me quickly and he shared something similar with my best friends: he was a baseball card fanatic too.

Professor Skuba began by describing the 'accidental' origins of sports marketing: baseball cards. As I'd come to find out, originally designed as protection for the tobacco in cigarettes, baseball cards weren't really seen as a real product in and of themselves. And since baseball had a very entrepreneurial ownership group, it had alway been very open to branding partnerships before other sports teams had even considered it. This led to printing cards to be put into cigarettes that could then be sold and marketed to patrons at a baseball game.

As it turned out, baseball was truly the backbone of sports marketing and those *stupid* cards I grew up with were the real starting place.

* * *

Baseball has been described as "American as Apple Pie." It is such a classic, iconic sport and is definitively American. If you think about it, it represents your home, America - and above all, American pride. The first form of sports marketing was through baseball cards, specifically baseball trading cards. Turns out, a lot of companies used to print a baseball player on one side of the trading card, and the other side had an advertisement for their company.

In the late 1860s a sporting goods company named Peck and Snyder, printed baseball cards and started using them as advertisements for their products - the way they did that was that on one side they had the picture of a famous baseball team, and on the other side they had an ad. They were known as the first company to do that. These cards were seen as trade cards.

Trade cards were seen as a very smart marketing tactic because instead of being sold with a product, they were given away - kind of like flyers on a street corner. Companies that advertised on those cards got a lot more face time/face value with customers since their name was branded/marketed on the back of the team the collector likes (creating a positive association in the mind of the collector regarding that brand). Collecting trade cards became really popular in the next 20 years, where people started collecting them more and more and would have scrapbooks with those trade cards in them.

Trading cards ended up expanding past baseball, for instance nowadays you have Pokémon and more, but just like sports marketing, trading cards originated through Baseball.

Topps Bubble Gum was huge in the sports marketing industry during baseball times. In the early 1950s, Topps was one of the biggest baseball card producers. However, they had their own twist - they sold baseball cards *inside* their packs of gum. Their baseball cards were numbered and they had collectible editions, and their cards are actually still sought after today, especially card #311 - the Mickey Mantle card - is the most sought after and expensive card they have.

Topps was very strategic in their marketing because they produced some of the most sought after cards but sold them only in packs of their bubble gum, requiring the consumer to purchase their product to get the desired baseball card. Topps became so successful and popular that they produced cards for big name companies like Kellogg's and Hostess.

Companies wanted their products to sell, that is why it was ingenious to introduce trading cards through baseball to entice new customers to buy their products. They wanted people to associate a good player to their brands, so it had a positive reinforcement around their brand, brand name, and products. They needed to be strategic about which players they put on their trade cards associated with their brand, because they didn't want to have a player that was disliked by everyone associated with their brand since can be perceived as a negative association in general.

Apart from the trade cards, baseball originated other forms of sports marketing tactics that are still in use today. The Louisville Slugger, a baseball bat maker, originated one of Nike's most used marketing strategies. They knew they had a lot of competition when they first entered the market, but all they wanted to do was distinguish themselves from everyone else.

You know that thing you learn in your marketing class that you hear the professor repeat over one hundred times - differentiation in the market is what sets you apart from everyone and can get you ahead in your industry??

Well, the only way for the Louisville Slugger to do so was for them to create some marketing strategy to set them apart from everyone else. What they did was they partnered with an actual athlete in order to say, "this is his baseball bat." So if consumers bought Louisville Slugger bats, it would say the athlete's name on it and he represented the face of the brand. They were smart enough to get a Hall of Fame baseball player - Honus Wagner. They used his name and face on the baseball bat.

This marketing strategy became a marketing practice that so many companies use nowadays, like Nike with their Michael Jordan line or Adidas with their Stan Smith line. Fun fact about the Stan Smith shoes that few know is that he is actually a really famous tennis player and not just the name of a trendy sneaker!

When I was explaining these strategies to one of my really good friends, Maryn, she asked me "How do you think they decided who to embody their brand?"

I realized this still applies a lot to marketing today, as much as it was applied to in the case of companies marketing towards baseball fans as well - it is always a fit with the company. Simply put, you want someone who represents your brand's values to represent your company. If we are talking about today, for example, Nike has Michael Jordan. He is such an iconic figure because he represents doing the impossible and making it possible, which is kind of what Nike tries to do with their "Just Do It" campaign.

I remember telling Maryn, "It's kind of the same way as to how Nike went about getting Michael Jordan, that's how the companies like the Louisville Slugger went about picking baseball players. Someone to echo their brand."

Yoo-Hoo chocolate milk came a little later in the game - around the late 1970s, 1980s. What they decided to do was get Yogi Berra, a baseball player who was known for being extremely sweet and kind to everyone, to represent their brand and their delicious chocolate milk. The chocolate milk was always the same, same formula, always really good, but they needed a little boost to get themselves on the market. Having Yogi Berra represent their brand was really what changed their entire image, and extremely interesting to me during my research, because people started really liking the chocolate milk once the Yogi ads came out. It became the brand of chocolate milk that everyone started drinking if they wanted to be seen as a good athlete. Their advertisements with Yogi Berra were so successful that they used him everywhere - they had some advertisements with him drinking it, televised advertisements in black and white, as well as a lot of print advertisements.

Wonder bread is another brand that echoed Yoo-Hoo chocolate milk's marketing strategies. Since baseball was such a popular sport, they had a lot of famous baseball players, like Mickey Mantle, who was one of the most iconic players to represent the bread. For Mickey Mantle to be seen saying, "I eat this bread," made their sales go through the roof.

Everyone is a sucker for a good brand that their favorite athlete likes, so Wonder bread sold extremely well. It makes sense that it is seen as the household, staple brand of bread because baseball is seen as that household, American sport.

The food industry is not the only industry that advertised through baseball. The tobacco industry was huge on advertising through baseball as well.

Just like trading cards were in bubble gum packs, trading cards with player's images were also placed into cigarette packs. Between the 1920s and the 1940s, every major league team had a cigarette sponsor, and baseball's greatest athletes all appeared in cigarette advertisements. For instance, Lou

Gehrig endorsed Camels, saying he could smoke as many as he pleased and created the slogan that Camels "don't get your wind."

However, as people started realizing that smoking was not good for your health, the Commissioner of Baseball forbade players to wear their baseball uniforms in any of the cigarette advertisements they were to appear in.

The home run of this chapter is that I learned how marketing tactics that emerged such a long time ago are still applied nowadays by extremely successful companies.

I would never have thought twice about how using an athlete to represent your brand, kind of like the Louisville Slugger bat makers did to have Honus Wagner, would impact, and inspire a brand like Nike when it was trying to differentiate itself on the market, later on. I always thought that it made sense that Michael Jordan represented Nike. However, if you think about it, it is very strategic on their end - by signing one of the greatest basketball players and giving him his own line, the Jordan line, Nike became iconic. They sell so much from that line, for instance Georgetown's basketball team is decked out from head to toe in the Jordan line (as shown in the picture below.)

It is incredibly interesting to see how that marketing practice is so active nowadays and not something that is outdated, since other marketing methods like radio advertisements are dying a lot, and print ads are not as predominant as YouTube or television ads nowadays, or even ads on social media that just pop up on the side of your screen. I think that it is fascinating to see how many of the strategies that were copied from baseball have been carried over and are still used today.

TAKEAWAY: BEGINNINGS OF SPORTS MARKETING

- Standard sports marketing strategies that are used today, started out as ways for companies simply to target a wider audience they knew would be paying attention: baseball fans

- Trade cards may no longer be used to market a specific brand or product, but they are still extremely sought after nowadays
  - For instance, Pokémon Trading cards have nothing to do with sports but are really popular
- Athletic sponsorships started out with baseball players and is today one of the biggest forms of sports marketing out there
  - An athlete playing their sport is an athlete showing their brand
  - You want an athlete whose brand represents your brand
    - You want that Cinderella glass slipper kind of magical fit

CHAPTER 4

EVOLUTION OF SPORTS MARKETING THROUGH NON-ATHLETIC BRANDS

———

"Packers star quarterback Aaron Rodgers is working with State Farm Insurance and Derek Jeter with Ford, but Kia and Subway hung millions on Blake Griffin as his star rose, while other unique partnerships have been realized throughout sports. Tennis star Rodger Federer partnered with Lindt Chocolates and Novak Djokovic with the emerging Japanese chain store Uniqlo. Golfer, Jim Furyk, even aligned himself with Five Hour Energy. Like Federer's and Djokovic's, endorsement deals, there are not exactly direct ties to golf or tennis. Then you have up and coming brands like MISSION Athletecare, who bring in athlete pairs like Serena Williams and Georges St. Pierre to not

just endorse but develop and invest equity in products like the Enduracool towel, and you see more how diverse brands are looking for pull in areas where they have not before."

INTERNATIONAL BUSINESS TIMES

✶ ✶ ✶

When I would come home from school the first thing I used to do was run towards the kitchen table where all our mail was properly placed. I used to sprawl it all out, sorting through everything to pull out all the magazines. I used to love pulling them out and shifting through the ads.

At the time, the *Got Milk* ads were everywhere.

Growing up, I *hated* milk. I refused to drink it. However, these *Got Milk* ads made me want to pour milk into my cereal.

Dad, can you get milk next time you go grocery shopping? I want it with my cereal.

I remember my dad was shocked. He didn't want to question why I decided to be healthy, since I was always on the shorter side growing up.

I used to rip out all the *Got Milk* ads with my favorite athletes and hang them up on my walls. I had all the ones you could think of: Michael Phelps, Serena Williams, Ana Ivanovic, Tom Brady, the US Olympic team in 2008, the list was not endless, but near.

I wanted to be just like them. I wanted to be an athlete. I needed to drink milk.

If I wanted to do well at swim practice on Sunday, I knew I needed to drink milk to be just like Michael Phelps. If I wanted to do well at tennis practice on Saturday, I needed to drink milk to be just like Serena Williams and Ana Ivanovic.

Sports marketing is unique: no other industry has *fans*.

Fans are loyal. They are not the average shifty consumer. Fans stick to a team; fans stick to a brand.

For companies to successfully target and acquire extremely loyal consumers, they needed to do so through sports. I love the aspect of sports bringing so many worlds together. Sports make dreams seem more attainable. That is why sports marketing is invaluable to companies who want to target the dreamers out there, the loyal fans, the ones who will buy a brand because there is meaning behind it. Sports marketing is personal.

Brands not related to sports marketing saw that and decided to venture into sports marketing. The pay-off has been absolutely worth it for those companies.

"When you think about sports marketing, it should be all the companies who have used sports to market themselves."

CHARLES J. SKUBA

To be honest, I had always thought that this was much simpler - sports companies used sports marketing to market themselves. But what I came to realize is that was far from the truth. Turns out any company can be a sports marketer and some of the brands spending the most on sports would surprise you.

"Coca Cola is one of the biggest sports marketers out there." Skuba said.

What? A drink that isn't necessarily the healthiest for an athlete to drink, is one of the biggest sports marketers out there? Okay...

Coca Cola's strategy, according to Skuba, is to make the consumer feel good and smile. For any Mad Men fans out there, you'll recognize this quote: "Advertising is based on one thing: happiness."

And Skuba had a point. Sports marketing doesn't necessarily

need to show the *physical* aspect of the sports as long as it shows the 'feel good' and happy aspects of sports.

"If a company has a target audience," he continued, "you need to know what sports they like and target that specific sport and its audience." For Coca Cola, their audience is much broader and wider yet they have been able to skillfully manage their marketing efforts to continue to acquire by targeting different consumers through different sports throughout different eras.

If, for example, Coke wants to target Europeans, then soccer is a really smart strategy. If they want to target Americans, football or baseball. Or targeting specific athletes by gender, race, or even age. Coke has a wide variety of consumers and they have successfully gone the extra mile to target everyone.

Coca Cola's marketing team is always churning their brains for a new innovative advertisement.

One of Coke's recent successful ad campaigns was the 2016 Rio Olympics ad, *What Does Gold Feel Like?* It just really emanated the team spirit and aspect of sharing a Coke with your teammates, sharing a Coke with those around you, and being extremely happy no matter how the score ends up at the end of the day - hopefully getting the Gold. The ad leaves you with such a positive feeling after watching it. You think that you like Coke even if you don't drink Coke.

They have been really good at adapting towards different cultures. That is why Coca Cola is such a global brand instead of local brand, like most of the baseball companies when sports marketing first started.

Professor Skuba said that they know how to target their audience really well. He talked about how his absolute favorite ad was the Mean Joe Greene ad.

If you haven't heard of it, it is an ad centered around a football player, Mean Joe Greene, who just came out of one of their games, and a little kid is there asking him questions. At first he is not very responsive but he is very nice about it. Then the little kid hands him his Coke so that Mean Joe Greene gets energy again, and he repays him by giving him his sweaty jersey.

What really made this ad successful was how the little boy was so happy after that interaction. Coke's goal is to make people happy, feel good, and smile, which is exactly what that ad does.

According to Skuba, another big sports marketer is Wheaties. *That's funny because I had always associated it with my grandfather since he used to eat those all the time for breakfast before switching to Special K when he was trying to lose weight.*

Skuba used to work for Wheaties in their sports marketing

department - fun fact: he actually worked on the Bruce Jenner campaign! He said that Wheaties always wanted to have an Olympic champion to represent the *Breakfast of Champions*.

How did they go about picking who was on their box? "Picking whoever was seen as the champion at the time" was what Skuba told me. "Actually, apart from Coca Cola, Wheaties might be one of the oldest, yet most tactful, sports marketers of all time."

When I was looking Wheaties up, I found that they had a 1920s box with Lou Gehrig, one of the most famous baseball players back in the day, on it. He was actually the first athlete to be featured on a Wheaties box. Wheaties is one of the first sports marketers that didn't use baseball trading cards.

To my own surprise, sports marketing can even be done through blogs.

During one of my work shifts, I remember sitting curled up in a ball on my chair repeatedly writing something, then deleting it, for this chapter. I cracked my back then turned around to see one of my coworkers staring at me. He told me I needed to take a break and get back to it with a fresh mind.

My coworker, Dan Kreytak is an extremely passionate photographer.

He was itching to tell me about this event he went to in Miami and started showing me the pictures he took at that event. One of the pictures he pulled up caught my eye but he kept scrolling.

No go back!

I immediately asked him to describe that event and send me the picture of himself at the event - Copa Basel. Solely based on Dan's pictures, it looked like an entirely Adidas sponsored event with only soccer fanatics there.

Copa Basel was celebrating a soccer blog called Kicks to the Pitch. The event was really special because it combined art and soccer fans to celebrate all things "Copa." Not only did Adidas help sponsor the event, but so did EA Sports and Heineken beer.

In the picture below of Dan, you can see a poster of Adidas sneakers, an Adidas jersey, Dan holding a pair of Adidas soccer cleats, as well as a Heineken beer in his hands.

This event was a combination of non-athletic brands all coming together to celebrate an art gallery, a soccer blog, and a charity to donate shoes to Soles4Souls - a non-profit global social enterprise committed to fighting poverty through the collection and distribution of shoes and clothing.

This event exemplifies how sports can bring so many different people together for both, a great cause and a good time. By partnering with this event, Adidas gained more fans and customers. Adidas was at the center of it, showcasing new shoes, as well as offering a free, limited-edition jersey for whoever donated a pair of unworn Adidas shoes to the event. Talk about branding at its finest.

This event not only makes companies like Adidas and Heineken favorable to a wider audience, but also proves that events are really one-of-a-kind marketing for companies.

It is money well spent to acquire a wider audience, while leaving a much more favorable impression in everyone's minds. The event left me with a more positive association with Adidas just by knowing they partnered with this event.

Consumer behavior is all psychological, and Adidas strategically targeted consumers by targeting their emotions and passions through this event.

TAKEAWAY: MILLENNIALS SHAPE TODAY'S INDUSTRY

- Millennials have been companies' biggest reason for the shift in sports marketing
  - Millennials have been told they are special and they can get anything they want
    - *Alright, how do we target them?*
  - The answer is quite simple: target what millennials like (sports, athletes, apparel...) and they will come to you
- Millennials love engaging with social media because it releases dopamine - a feel good chemical
  - Dopamine is highly addictive, and gives the same feeling

that smoking and drinking does, that is why millennials turn to social media - to get that addictive feel good feeling
  - ◆ Companies know to target millennials through social media because millennials are attached to their phones
- Millennials are embracing non-apparel products endorsed by sports fans whether they realize it or not
  - ◆ For instance, if Michael Phelps is seen wearing Beats headphones and tweets about it or posts an Instagram picture wearing them, his entire following will want to want to purchase it
    - ▪ *As millennials, we seek satisfaction through material things*
- This marketing strategy allows more companies to target and connect with a much wider audience and fan-base
  - ◆ Sports fans are *loyal*, by targeting these specific people, companies are acquiring loyal consumers
- Coca Cola is not a healthy beverage, athletes do not reach for Coke to replenish their electrolytes after a tough workout, they reach for Powerade or Gatorade
  - ◆ Even though we have a generation that is shifting and focusing on health a lot, Coca Cola will not lose its consumers because of the power of marketing
    - ▪ They have found that sweet spot when it comes to targeting their consumers through their marketing that will allow them to stick around for a while, at least until they find a formula that is less sugary and healthier

PART 2

SPORTS MARKETING'S EVOLUTION

CHAPTER 5

SPORTS MARKETING IN SPORTING EVENTS AND THROUGH SPORTS TEAMS

"In 2014 Manchester United signed its seven-year, $559 million contract with Chevrolet. That $80 million-per-year payout more than doubled what the team was getting from its prior jersey sponsorship and blew away the rest of the field. Even two years later the next largest corporate partnership, Chelsea's $57 million-per-year deal with Yokohama Rubber, is well behind.

"And yet the top spot on our list of the sport's biggest sponsorship winners belongs to a different team: Real Madrid. Los Blancos had actually lagged behind the leaders as recently as a year ago, but an astounding ten-year, $1.6 billion deal with Adidas swiftly *brought that to an end. The team now makes some $192 million from its jerseys each year (and that's despite an Emirates Airways partnership that seemed undervalued when it was signed in 2013). Toss in a new $28 million-per-year stadium naming rights agreement with the United Arab Emirates, which will rename Santiago Bernabeu once its renovations are completed, and you've got the biggest sponsorship haul in the sport."*

- FORBES, MAY 11, 2016

* * *

My favorite thing is to watch European soccer games with my dad. The day before Thanksgiving we were switching between the UEFA Champions league match where FCBarcelona was playing against the Celtics, and the Paris Saint Germain vs. Arsenal match. While watching I noticed so many subtle yet effective sports marketing tactics that companies I would have never associated with soccer, used to diffuse their brand's name during the game.

I never considered sporting events as one of the largest ways in which brands can promote themselves.

The biggest thing I noticed was that Arsenal's jerseys had the Puma logo on it, and was completely baffled to see that Puma even penetrated the soccer market.

Are you sure dad? I thought Puma was a dying brand. He was sure. *That's amazing.*

He continued to tell me that Puma had actually unveiled their new body hugging jerseys during the last World Cup.

So, kind of like the catwalk reveal of soccer jerseys?

* * *

For the Puma/Arsenal deal, Arsenal chose to go with Puma after 20 years with Nike.

Twenty years with Nike and they could just switch brands so easily??

Simply put, the deal with Puma provided them with a much more significant sum. Paired with the Emirates contract, these deals gave them more spending power in terms of acquiring stronger players for the team, or increasing players' pay, or even what benefits the team can get. *That's so much money.*

However, this is a two-way street, as are most sports marketing sponsorship deals, and the deal with Arsenal brought a lot of new sales to Puma. *Oh well that makes a lot of sense!*

The important thing to keep in mind when it comes to any

marketing deal is that its main goal is to acquire more customers, increase current customer loyalty, retention, as well as increase market share and recognition.

* * *

Similarly to Puma, another thing that shocked me was seeing New Balance's logo on the Celtic jerseys.

Only Steve Jobs can pull off New Balance!

Actually, New Balance is not only making a trendy comeback, but I found the same thing happened for Celtic regarding their jerseys: they switched from Nike as well.

Many teams were switching from Nike - who could provide them with more money than they actually were - for deals with other lesser famous brands (i.e. New Balance for Celtic or Puma for Arsenal) that would benefit them in the short-term and long-term a lot more.

Smaller teams are trying to get more out of sponsorship deals that they make, that is why they have been switching to brands that are willing to provide them more money and a better contract deal.

* * *

Another thing I had always known about but never really questioned was the fact that on FCBarcelona's jerseys always had in large bold print "Qatar Foundation." My dad told me that in 2010 Qatar Foundation had signed a 5-year deal with FCBarcelona to sponsor them, and that the deal was worth $220 million.

Oh my God that is SO much money.

He told me that they extended that deal for one more year once the contract was up for $90 million. *Jeez but it does make sense that they would want their name plastered in such a large font over the center of the jerseys of one of the greatest soccer teams right now.*

This is the exact same case for Arsenal, where the players' jerseys had in the same large bold print previously mentioned, "Fly Emirates." In 2004, Emirates signed a $100 million contract with Arsenal for a 15-year deal, and renewed that deal in 2012 for $150 million dollars to extend the contract until the end of the 2018-2019 season.

Why are these deals worth so much money? What is so special about this form of sports marketing?

With these questions flowing around my mind, I got really curious and decided to look further into the Qatar and

Emirates sponsorships. I found an article named "Gulf air-lines build awareness, one sports sponsorship at at time," that answered all my questions about why airlines are spending such hefty sums sponsoring soccer teams.

The article states that these Gulf airlines are a lot newer on the market than their predecessors who have higher name recognition. Because of that, they realized that sports was the easiest way for their brand name to reach the most eyeballs on the market.

These companies sponsor more than just soccer, they have large sponsorship deals with Formula One, Rugby teams, Tennis Championships, Golf Tournaments, Horse Racing, and Sailing.

That seems like a pretty large margin to cover...

These sponsorship deals do more than simply benefit the airways themselves. They help cover the rather large salaries of the soccer players of those teams.

When I looked for further information on how much money is poured into soccer sponsorships, I saw that it goes beyond simply the name recognition on jerseys, for some teams, it also involves naming rights of the stadium, as well as a pos-sible shareholder value. For instance, Bayern Munich sold its stadium naming rights to Allianz, who is also a minority shareholder and holds a 30-year contract with them.

I had never really looked at these types of sponsorship deals as a two-way street before, but it was really interesting to see how this is kind of like the version of what one may be able to inaptly call the "sports circle of life."

* * *

Apart from such hefty contracts, something I also noticed while watching the soccer matches with my dad was that an interesting mix of companies advertise their brand names on the electronic banners around the stadium. The most compelling one to me was seeing Heineken's name popping up all around the stadium with their tag-line. When I questioned my dad further on it, he told me they are a Dutch brand. Seeing that they were advertising their brand for the Celtic vs. FCBarcelona game, I thought it was actually a very tactful move on their end. Targeting not only the Scottish who were most likely watching it, rooting for their team, but also trying to get their brand name out to the Catalan, who most likely drink Estrella Damm.

They are targeting the consumer's behavior through subconscious recognition that will register in their heads at a future time, so that they are more likely to reach for a Heineken beer next time they watch soccer, instead of another brand.

Why would a brand want to choose soccer to advertise with, rather than another sport though?

This question reminded me of a conversation I once held unexpectedly with an Uber driver, whose name was Happy. His name was really fitting for his personality. The day of my ride there happened to be a football game that evening.

Are you going to watch the game tonight? He asked me.

Instead of ending the conversation with a simple, shy "no," something in me decided it was better to hold a conversation with him.

No I'm not, I'm more of a soccer person. I grew up watching it with my dad.

He told me that he loved soccer because no matter what is going on around the world, it unites people together to play one game together. *It really shows sportsmanship.* I never thought of soccer in such a deep sense. "With the World Cup, you watch teams who represent countries that have fought wars against each other, but once they are both on the field, they are a family, regardless of whether or not they are playing the match against each other."

As Phil Knight said in his memoir, *Shoe Dog*, "When sports are at their best, the spirit of the fan merges with the spirit of the athlete and in that convergence, in that transference, is the oneness that the mystics talk about." When I am watching intense matches, I get so involved that I physically ache when I see a player hit the ground, get hit in the face by a ball flying at god knows what speed, or get injured.

There is a sense of unity when it comes to sports, and whether or not you are the spectator or the player, we all have the same goals and are all together in this crazy community. You feel the pain of loss; you feel the elation of a win.

In sports, you celebrate the victories, and seek for a shoulder to lean on during times when you feel defeated.

* * *

The whole aspect of everyone coming together over one sport because it creates a sense of community, is so crucial in understanding why a brand picks a certain sport to use as their means of marketing rather than another.

In choosing a sport like soccer, as a brand, you are associating yourself to a team sport, a community, and a family. By sponsoring a sports team, you are hoping and trying to convince in a subtle manner, consumers to join your family and community, as well as team, when they choose to purchase your brand's products over another brand's.

It is much harder to properly choose to associate your brand with a singular athlete rather than a sports team. For instance, Rolex sponsors one of the greatest tennis players in history, Roger Federer, but by doing so, they had to make sure they chose a tasteful player that represented their elite and classy brand. You wouldn't associate a watch with a sport, however Roger Federer is such a classic, iconic, and above all, historic figure, who represents an equally classic, iconic, and historic brand.

It is about the most strategic and somewhat magical of fits because you want to avoid having a sponsorship that blows up in your face.

* * *

I am that dad who gets up and cheers, or even yells, at soccer games. I just get really into it. I usually scream when someone kicks the ball to the wrong side of the field, "to who???" If you are a soccer dad, let's watch a game together!! If you aren't a soccer dad, I apologize for getting really heated during games.

I found the perfect match in my best friend Maria Bianculli. She is exactly the equivalent of me at soccer games, but at basketball games. Maria grew up watching Georgetown basketball games with her dad.

I could be considered as someone who is "obsessed with sports." Maria is the opposite. Honestly, that is probably one of the reasons that we get along so well because opposites attract. That, and she has seen me at my worst at Georgetown soccer games and has stuck around. Thank you for that.

Because she grew up watching basketball games, the way I watched soccer games, I decided to ask her what she thought of when she thought of sports marketing. I wanted to see if it would follow my theory that what people pay attention to when it comes to marketing, varies based on their passions and interests.

She said, "To be honest, none have ever stuck out to me so much for me to remember it. I mean I'm sure there have been some that I really like. I guess I really like the videos that open Georgetown Basketball games, those get me in my feelings."

Why do those videos get you in your feelings/stick out to you? "It is probably a mix of the environment its played in honestly. All the lights go out in the Verizon Center and you know the game is about to start. The video gets you so so pumped and makes you think Georgetown is the coolest place in the world. I probably really like it because I grew up going to the games and I've seen the videos as they've changed since I was young."

I had never thought of that perspective. I never thought that sports marketing could apply to a school like Georgetown, but it does make sense. A significant portion of Georgetown's revenue comes from sports, specifically one of our strongest teams: basketball.

Georgetown Basketball has had a long history and Georgetown has always been known for it. I never thought of how it could be marketed since I thought they were synonymous, but now that Maria has pointed it out, it does add a layer to the onion of what sports marketing is.

* * *

When conducting research on NBA sponsorships, I stumbled across the craziest of findings: Anheuser-Busch and State Farm are the leading sponsors of NBA teams.

It baffled me to think that not a company like Nike that sponsors the jerseys or the Jordan sneakers the players wear, but a beer company is the largest sponsor of NBA teams.

Not only that but the top of the sponsorship list for NBA teams is followed by Gatorade, MillerCoors - another beer company, and Geico - another insurance company. NBA sponsorships make soccer sponsorships seem trivial in comparison - during the 2015-2016 season, NBA sponsorships totaled $799 million for 30 teams, and that sum was up 8.1% from the previous season according to IEG research. State Farm is the leading sponsor, where 83% of teams have some sort of sponsorship with the insurance company.

What really grabbed my attention was the fact that these brands, apart from Gatorade and Adidas, really had nothing to do with sports. I was also really shocked to see the dominance of both malt companies and insurance companies. Completely different from the soccer industry in what kinds of companies choose to invest their funds in for marketing.

∗ ∗ ∗

Something else I found absolutely fascinating is that apart from the incredibly large revenues basketball teams are receiving from sponsorships, they found a way to make even more revenue by allowing shirt sponsorship advertising space starting the 2017-2018 playing season.

This is literally following in soccer's footsteps in order for teams to acquire even more revenue than they are currently generating. I found that to be absolutely baffling.

NBA commissioner Adam Silver said that "Jersey sponsorships

provide deeper engagement with partners looking to build a unique association with our teams, and the additional investment will help grow the game in exciting new ways."

I have found this to be true when it comes to marketing sponsorships on soccer jerseys. The NBA/basketball as a whole seems to embrace this older marketing strategy adapted a while ago by soccer teams. Not only that, but in June 2016, the NBA made a deal with Nike for $1 billion to have the Nike swoosh logo on the right shoulder of all 30 NBA teams.

So much more money and strategic subliminal sports marketing messages that I never previously would have looked into is involved, which is still mind blowing to me.

✶ ✶ ✶

This goes to show that marketing strategies never get outdated, especially regarding sponsorships. They just get adapted and better with time and technology enhancements.

✶ ✶ ✶

When you ask most people what their favorite sporting event is, the most common event you hear is The Olympics. Do you know why the Olympics started? I could tell you that I didn't. I found out the origins of the Olympics when I was chatting my dad's head off about how cool the ads were this past year.

Did you know that the origins of the Olympics Games were to foster sports rather than war among different Greek city-states? He asked me.

No. I genuinely had no idea...

How incredible is it that sports was used to create some form of peace??

I decided to look into how the Olympics fostered peace among people, and found that it played an extremely influential role in the 2012 Olympics. I read that sports have been used since the Olympics started out as a way to promote peace and international cooperation.

How cool is that??

Sports has not only changed the relations between countries through events in the subtlest of ways, but so has its marketing.

I cannot imagine how crazy the Olympic village must look throughout the events leading up to the Olympics, or even during the events itself. It must be absolutely insane with brand names and enlarged logos all over the place. The Olympics are a multi-billion-dollar industry for marketers. It is a huge opportunity for companies to get face value and face time with potential customers, or acquire new customers through new sponsorship deals with athletes.

One of the biggest and most famous sponsors during the Olympics is actually Coca Cola. Coca Cola holds the longest standing relationship with the Olympic Games. Their support at the Olympics actually dates back to the Summer Games of 1928 in Amsterdam, where the drink was first offered to athletes and observers. Currently, Coca Cola pays the International Olympic Committee (IOC) about $100 million in the four-year timespan between Games to get the title "Worldwide Olympic Partner" and be able to advertise directly at the event.

Coca Cola's advertisements are really what give them the title of greatest sports marketing according to Professor Skuba. Their ads leave you with that same good feeling that you get when your favorite team wins, some sort of faith, satisfaction, and above all, full heart.

Clear eyes, full hearts, can't lose.

Not Coca Cola's motto, but their ads definitely leave you feeling that way. I am positive if I went around right now asking everyone their favorite Coca Cola ad, they could immediately come up with it. Professor Skuba's is not an Olympic related one, but nonetheless a sports related one, and he knew *exactly* which one was his favorite.

Procter & Gamble are also one of the biggest sports marketers and presences at the Olympics. Just like Coca Cola, P&G is also part of the few companies that pays the International Olympic Committee (IOC) about $100 million in the four year timespan between Games to get the title "Worldwide Olympic Partner" and be able to advertise directly with the event. They are known for their "Thank You Mom" ads.

To quote Maria, *those ads just get me in my feelings.*

Their ads are so strong at connecting the viewers' emotions in such a subtle way to their products that the consumer is inevitably going to have such a positive perspective of the brand, and later on recall how great that ad was, and therefore purchase P&G products because of that.

Have you ever not shed a tear or have your eyes water watching one of P&G's "Thank You Mom" ads for the Olympics?

Because as strong as I would like to think I am, boy do those ads get me with their strong emotions.

An interesting finding in an Ad Week article that I stumbled upon was the Olympic Rule 40. It was announced by the

IOC in February 2015, and stated that Olympic athletes were now allowed to appear in generic advertising that does not explicitly mention the games or use any Olympic intellectual property (those qualify as the Olympic rings, using specific terms, etc.) It is widely known that Nike is the official brand that sponsors all Olympic athletes' gear, and because of that Under Armour was one of the smartest companies to benefit from Rule 40.

Under Armour came up with their "Rule Yourself" campaign, that are less than two-minute advertisements that show the U.S. women's gymnastics team training really hard, as well as one with Michael Phelps (that ended up winning an award at Cannes), which shows him training incredibly hard as well. Both Under Armour ads followed Rule 40 restrictions and were launched within the time frames delineated by the IOC.

The Olympics' marketing rules are so harsh to non-partner companies, that brands needs to be so strategic about their moves around the Olympics to be able to get their name around without doing so in an illegal manner. Regardless of strict rules and the politics behind them, the ads that come out of the Olympics are part of the most awe-inspiring, motivating, and goose bump inducing ads I have ever seen. I always wonder what was someone's thought process when creating such incredible ads.

TAKEAWAY: LET'S GO WATCH
THE BASKETBALL GAME

- The last thing anyone thinks of when they are going to watch a basketball game is what companies or brands will be targeting them
  - It is really quite simple: you go because you want to support your favorite team
- Now think of it this way, everywhere you turn you see "Giant is the official sponsor of the Washington Wizards"
  - As a Wizards fan, you are going to subconsciously register this and have a more favorable opinion of Giant next time you are going grocery shopping
- Sporting events are the best places for a brand to get their name out their on electronic banners or on the plastic cups people are drinking beer out of
  - The more eyes that see your brand name, the more recognition you will get next time
    - This targets multiple key senses: brand resonance, atti-tudinal attachment, building a sense of community, and active engagement within the consumer's behavior

CHAPTER 6

RICHARD POORMAN

———

"Under Armour's signature story represents its key brand cores of innovation, not to mention its core target of athletes concerned with performance. Founder and CEO Kevin Plank was a football player at Maryland in the mid-1990s when he became frustrated by his cotton t-shirt that got wet, heavy and uncomfortable during workouts. To solve for his problem of being the self-proclaimed "sweatiest player on the field," Plank created undergarments with materials borrowed from women's lingerie materials that would "wick and dry" the sweat from his clothing.

"Plank created a new subcategory of clothing that stays fresh and dry – and dominated it. Today, Under Armour has a 75% market share. The signature story continues to provide authenticity and interest to the brand. Take a look at the Tough Mudder and

Ridge Reaper stories on their website for exhilarating stories of #IWILL.

"Creating energy and providing substance behind the "I will" message is not a strategy so much as the brand's culture. Among their branded innovative products are Infrared technology that recirculates heat around the wearer's body, Coldback technology designed to reflect heat and keep athletics cool in the sun, and MagZip technology which allows a zipper to be pulled with one hand."

DAVID AACKER, PROFIT

* * *

You know that really cliché saying *everything happens for a reason*? My parents are the kings and queens of saying that whenever I get sad about an outcome I didn't want out of a situation. I can give you a couple examples:

1. Getting denied from applying early decision to Vanderbilt University - *don't worry, everything happens for a reason!* Of course, I have never been happier to get denied from a place because I got the best of outcomes by going to Georgetown, but obviously, at the time that was not what I wanted to hear at all.

2. Getting job rejections - *everything happens for a reason honey,*

don't be sad about it, you are stronger person from each rejection, it's for the best. I'm sure, but that feeling still sucks. A lot.

* * *

Today, I learned that that saying is not only applicable to less than desirable outcomes in my life, but also to the greatest of them. Today is the day I met Richard Poorman.

A couple months ago I signed up for a really random half marathon in Fairfax, Virginia because I wanted something else to train for to keep challenging myself. I know most people stop after one and are happy with what they accomplished, but I strongly believe that the more I do, the more I can mentally and physically challenge myself, the more I will grow as a person. With my half marathon tomorrow, I completely forgot to go pick up my race pack while studying for finals, and realized I had to go today, no matter how much studying I had left to do. I finished my last run before d-day approached, showered, and while my laundry was in, got into an Uber to a place I have never heard of before, called Metro Run & Walk.

I was a little nervous while on the drive over. I don't know why. It could have been because I was nervous it would be too cold in the morning before my half marathon. Or the fact that someone told me running your second half marathon is a lot harder than your first because you know what to expect.

Regardless of what the root of my nerves was, my brain was all over the place.

Once I found the little running store, I walked in straight to the table that had a sign that read "Packet Pick Up Here." I got my bib, race shirt, and pins. Usually, I would have walked out of the store because I got what I came for. For some reason I started walking around the store and saw that two of the employees, one older man, and one college aged man, were both watching the Navy vs. Army football game. It was just as the game was starting up. Both of them were enthusiastically asking customers who were walking in who they were rooting for. A woman said her husband was an Army veteran, so she had to root for them, even though they had a 14 year losing streak. The older man said he was rooting for Navy but did not give any pretext or feel as though he needed to justify why he wanted them to win, like the woman had.

I heard the older man comment on Navy's uniforms saying "they are Under Armour!" Naturally, being the sports geek that I am, I had to linger around. I slowly got closer to the television they were watching from, and the older man asked me if I wanted a chair and hot chocolate to sit with them. I got really nervous and said, "Oh no thank you, I have to go back and study for my finals." But that answer got me roped in a conversation with the younger man, who told me he went to school not far from Virginia Tech.

I genuinely could not tell you how, but I found myself telling the older man about how I am writing a book on the evolution of sports marketing and the next thing I knew, I had a pad of paper in my hands and a pen. The older man's name is Richard Poorman. He honestly has to be one of the most interesting and fascinating people I have ever met in my life thus far.

Richard Poorman is a retired Navy veteran - which makes sense as to why he was rooting for Navy in the football game. He saw the coat I was wearing said "Arctic Program" on it, and asked me if I have ever been to Antarctica. "I haven't" I said, deeply wishing I had so that I could tell him a cool story, but I looked down at my old gray shoes instead. He told me that when he was still in the Navy, he spent two years in Antarctica as an aerial photographer. He had this glimmer in his eyes that made me want to ask him his entire life story, but just took whatever he gave me because every word he said was already unbelievably interesting. He said they used to do penguin counts of the entire continent. He said taking the pictures took about 6 months total to take. What really intrigued me was how they actually counted all the penguins: he said they laid out a grid of all the pictures they took, and would count grid by grid, and labelled it all as they went, in order to keep track of everything.

I asked Mr. Poorman how he got into running. He told me that he spent 22 years in the Navy and when he retired, he absolutely hated running. He told me that he was hunting and fishing instead. His wife was in the Marine Corps in their public affairs department, and said that he had put on some weight and suggested he take up running. He was adamant on not running. However, his wife would not take no for an answer and they went to a shoe fitting together to get him a pair of running sneakers. After that, he fell in love with running. When I asked how he got into working at a running store, he said that he got really inquisitive about how he had gotten fitted, and started working at that shoe store every Saturday. He told me he then started working at Metro Run & Walk, which he saw as a small mom-and-pop, brick-and-mortar store that he loved. I could understand how he loved working there, it was small, but really friendly. I noticed during my time there that almost every single customer that walked through the store was a repeat customer and they all said some variation of "I am looking to get a shoe similar to the one you sold me a while back."

Mr. Poorman told me that Metro Run & Walk has been open for about 14 years but is really unique. He's been working there for about four years. What he loves about being there is that while other stores try to upsell the customer by trying to sell a shoe *with* something all the time, Metro Run & Walk does not do that. They work based on honesty and that seems to have worked in their favor since most of their business (about 70% of it) is repeat customers. They have a system that keeps track of what people wear to help figure out other pairs of sneakers they can buy if the model they like is no longer sold. He also said he loves how involved this small store is - they have about 8 races a year, where all the profit goes towards a non-profit in Fairfax.

I loved Mr. Poorman's passion for his job, which to be honest, I don't think he saw as a job himself. He saw it more as something he did because he loved the feeling of having done a customer well when they return asking for running shoes he previously got them fitted for. He kept saying that he *chose* to do this. He said that he is aware that small stores like Metro Run & Walk will probably close because of online businesses selling shoes at a much more discounted price. Mr. Poorman said something that resonated a lot with me: the shoe doesn't change, but the customers come back for store values and the relationships they developed with the employees. He said, "The biggest thing you can do for a customer is just to listen to them."

Mr. Poorman's knowledge about running was unreal to me. He looked at my feet and was like "what are you, a 6.5/7?" I was so shocked my jaw probably dropped to the ground. That was exactly my shoe size. How did he guess that by just looking at my baby-sized feet? I was so impressed and in awe. He was spitting really cool numbers about runners - he said that about 90% of runners get the same shoes when they need a new pair. He was really accurate about saying that runners are creatures of habit. As a runner, I believe that I too, am a creature of habit as well. His knowledge about running shoes went beyond anything I could fathom. He told me that all Asics sneakers were named after different clouds, and that the amount of gel (to increase cushioning) put in the shoe is what creates the difference in price between two pairs of sneakers.

I decided to pick his brain and ask him his thoughts on Nike. I was genuinely intrigued. In my eyes, I not only earned so much respect for this man I met and spent about two hours with, but looked up to him and his passion. He told me that in his opinion, Nike had functional apparel and average running shoes. He said that Nike apparel sells a lot, but whenever their sales tech comes in, they are pretentious about everything because they are aware that their brand is so sought after. He told me that is it hard to talk a young person into a non-Nike brand when it comes to running shoes. He said "they see the swoosh, and all they want is the swoosh." Having thoroughly read Phil Knight's memoir, Shoe Dog, I blurted "I think it is so weird that Nike was a company founded on a running shoe, yet it produces average running shoes." He laughed and said, "Do you want me to tell you why I think Nike took a set back when it comes to their running shoes? Michael Jordan." I looked at him, with my big eyes, open wider and larger than usually. He said that Nike sold because of him, so they chose to focus on him, and his line instead. It made sense. I just had never looked it at that way. Hearing the words come out of his mouth were like solving the world's greatest mystery, but they made so much sense.

I did not have to inquire further, he walked me to the men's shoe wall and pointed at the different Nike shoes. He said that the Nike representatives don't have to push their sneakers, "Because it is Nike. It's as simple as that." He continued to say, "Nike floods the market, it's all Nike all the time. They get the biggest name athletes, and people follow the swoosh." *Follow the swoosh.* That was all I needed. I always knew that athletic sponsors were huge for a company, I just never looked at it with that perspective. I thought to myself, "I clearly need more perspective on these things because everyone keeps shattering my views on everything."

While I had his attention, I decided to ask about his opinions on Under Armour. The first thing he said, "They are not a shoe company." I completely agreed. I was aware that Under Armour has been trying really hard to break into the shoe market, but has not had that breakthrough sneaker yet. He saw my dejected look, clearly knowing I liked Under Armour a lot, as the first words we had exchanged to each other were "Do you like Navy's uniforms?" and with twinkly eyes and a shy face I said, "I love Under Armour, so I am extremely biased here." He went on to say, "But their apparel is wonderful. I love their hunting gear. Their upstart is also incredible." Everyone loves a good story, and Mr. Poorman was no exception to falling as in love with Under Armour's underdog startup story, just as I had.

I left Metro Run & Walk and Mr. Poorman feeling eternally grateful for random encounters like the one I had today. I went in to get my race packet, but left with so much more than I ever expected to learn.

Mr. Poorman had captured the power of sports marketing. Jordan had forever changed Nike from an upstart running shoe company into the dominant shoe company period. But did the marketing supercede the product's qualities at a certain point? Poorman seemed to think so and as I was looked down at the Asics I was going to wear to my half marathon, I was pretty certain it had too.

And at the same time that little upstart company from Baltimore (well not so little) had a story that in many ways was like Nike before Nike was Jordan's Nike.

That's the power of sports marketing — the ability to transcend the quality of the products; the ability to ride the success of the world's greatest basketball player of all time; the ability to turn an apparel company into the biggest threat to Nike.

And that's why sports marketing is so powerful — it takes the magic of sports and turns those stories into legends.

That's why I am so fascinated by the sports marketing industry. It's the upstart of companies like Nike and Under Armour even when there are already dominant players in the industry like Adidas and Puma. Like my best friend Maria loves to tell me, *Just because there's a goalie, doesn't mean you can't score*. It's the company that still hasn't let marketing trump product. And it's the culture of athletes competing against the bigger, stronger, faster dominant player in the field.

All that from a two-hour conversation with a guy who sells running shoes. Definitely happened for a reason...

Not only was yesterday a crazy day for me, but Army ended up winning against Navy, breaking their 14 year losing streak, defying all odds.

Even though Under Armour is not a shoe company, Nike is a shoe brand. As my friend Rodney told me, "I like Nike because it is clean cut, classic, iconic, and not flashy." Nike and Under Armour have both revolutionized the sports apparel industry in so many ways, especially with incredible ad campaigns and slogans that are written on shirts everywhere, and sprawled on stickers on people's laptops everywhere. From *Just Do It* to *Protect This House* both companies have changed the way sports marketing is done for sports apparel companies.

CHAPTER 7

BRANDS LIKE NIKE AND UNDER ARMOUR CHANGING THE WAY CAMPAIGNS ARE DONE

During the start of finals study days, I was sitting in the library in black Under Armour sweatpants, a black Under Armour sweatshirt, and black Nike sneakers.

I don't think I have ever been as focused as I was in that moment, when a damp paper ball hit me on the shoulder and fell on my lap.

I looked up and two of my good guy friends, Ben and Sagar,

were sitting at a table not far from me started yelling "Nerd! Nerd!"

Ben looked at me and said "Pick a team Yas!" I was really confused until Sagar pointed out that I was dressed in Under Armour but had Nike sneakers on.

Why do I need to pick a team?

Telling someone to pick between Nike and Under Armour is like telling someone to pick one ice cream flavor for the rest of their lives and stick to it.

That is just cruel.

The reason that Under Armour has been able to be so successful is because people like me don't "pick a team." We love both companies and want to get their products because they are exactly what we are looking for. Though sitting right there in a full on bloutfit - my take on the groutfit - I could have been an ad straight out of Runner's World or SHAPE magazine.

I left the library not long after to go to my IM basketball game. I usually love IM games, but that day I just did not want to be there. Of course, both teams had 9 players, but something crazy that I noticed was that all 18 players, except for one, were wearing Nike sneakers to the game. All the guys, again except for one, had Nike shorts on. All three referees on the court had Nike sneakers on as well. I was no exception. I too was wearing Nike sneakers.

At one point in the game, one of the guys on the opposing team, Ryan, yelled out "You miss 100% of the shots you don't take." In that moment, his comment made me zone out. I had no idea why but I completely checked out of the game. It just really got me thinking about sports, about this book, about my future... I felt so bad because I was running back and forth on the court, but was not actually present. It is as if I blacked out and somehow appeared on the court as one of my teammates yelled "Yas! Come up! Not there! Left!"

As I got onto the bench, I immediately took out the first book I had and started jotting my observations down. Everyone was judging me for doing what they thought was "homework" during the game, but in reality I was so intrigued by how many people were wearing Nike on all 4 courts. In a game happening on the courts facing the ones I was playing on, only two people of the 19 were not wearing Nike sneakers. I recognized one was Saucony sneakers, and the other had Brooks running shoes. Why running shoes to a basketball game? The answer was beyond me, but then again, not everyone is a sneaker fanatic like I am. Maybe not fanatic? *Am I just crazy obsessed with sports? I don't think I want to think about that right now.*

One of my teammates asked me what I was doing when I was furiously writing because she was genuinely curious. I was kind of really happy and grateful she did not think that I was crazy when I told her to look at how everyone was wearing Nike sneakers except for 3 people out of 38. That is 79% of people on the court wearing Nike. I waited silently for her reaction, and she was actually amazed by it and thought it was just as cool as I thought it was.

Maybe she was not as excited as I was about this, but it just went to show that Nike is really dominant in the shoe industry. Which is crazy and amazing at the same time because everyone doubted Phil Knight when he first started his company.

Phil was right - belief in something really does go a long way.

* * *

Sports marketing started with baseball, Nike started with running, and Under Armour started with football. Again, we all have a story, and we all started somewhere.

Truth in Marketing.

This concept is so important. You know how when you see an ad, you hope not to be deceived by it?

Brands like Nike and Under Armour thrive because they build their companies based on honesty. In his book, *Shoe Dog*, Phil Knight talks about how people trusted Nike and Nike's shoes because they were always honest. They wanted to put the consumer first and not sales or revenue first. Under Armour became so successful because their strategy was to be honest the entire way through - telling the consumer everything they were wearing and where it came from. To be successful, you need to be honest and humble.

Stay humble, stay hopeful.

* * *

My dad is what you can definitely call one of those drivers who does not respect speed limits unless necessary. He thinks they are more of a suggestion than anything else. I remember driving with him once and commented on how many speed cameras were set into place, "it is probably because of how you speed all the time, dad." He laughed and said, "speed limits are for other people, not for your dad."

Speed limits are for other people, not for your dad.

Pushing yourself past what you think you can do, and past where everyone else thinks they should stop, because it leads to greatness.

If Phil Knight and Kevin Plank gave up, and did not push past the imaginary speed limits where people don't pursue their dreams, no one would be walking around wearing Air Jordan or Curry sneakers. No one would be wearing revolutionary Heat or Cold Gear, sweat-wicking shirts, TB12 recovery sleepwear, or flyknit sneakers.

Nike and Under Armour have not only revolutionized the sports apparel industry, but also the sports marketing industry. They both have inspiring stories that brought them to us, but failed so hard, and so many times, before they became the big giants in the industries. For every great athlete, you can fall 100 times, but you need the greatness and determination that it takes to get up 101 times.

No one is great overnight, you need to work for it.

If Phil Knight did not create Nike, and Kevin Plank did not create Under Armour, someone else would have come up with something similar.

If not you, then who? If not now, then when?

* * *

That's a swoosh. It's the sound of someone going past you.

- PHIL KNIGHT, *SHOE DOG*

Nike was founded in 1964, under the name Blue Ribbon Sports by Phil Knight and Oregon head track coach, Bill Bowerman. The company initially served as a distributor of running shoes by a Japanese company named Onitsuka Tiger, which is nowadays known as Asics. After a lot of trials and tribulations, in 1971, Blue Ribbon Sports launched their own brand of shoes and needed a new name for it if they were going to sell it onto the market. Knight hired a design student, Carolyn Davidson, to come up with the logo for $35, and after many options, she came up with what is now known as the Nike *Swoosh*. Funny thing is, Knight had said, "Well, I don't love it, but maybe it will grow on me."

Now that they had a logo, all they needed was a name. Knight wanted to name the brand *Dimension Six* but it did not stick well with anyone that heard it. Jeff Johnson, known as Blue Ribbon Sports, as well as Nike's, first employee actually came up with Nike. *What's a Nike?* It is the Greek winged goddess of victory. Everything that the company represented in a four letter word.

BRANDS LIKE NIKE AND UNDER ARMOUR CHANGING THE WAY CAMPAIGNS ARE DONE · **127**

*"Running for pleasure, running for exercise, running for endor-
phins, running to live better and longer - these things were
unheard of."*

- PHIL KNIGHT, *SHOE DOG*

Nike went through a lot before it became known as the biggest, dominant player in the sports industry. However, they
were extremely smart and strategic about it the entire time
they were starting out the company. Nike stood by what they
believed in - they were founded by someone extremely passionate who had a lot of faith in his idea, no matter what
anyone else, even his father said. Nike was founded based on
absolute faith in an idea that went a really long way.

That feeling is still applicable nowadays in whatever Nike does
due to the way that their marketing has so many advertisements that try to show people working towards something and
have inspirational tag-lines that kind of echo the sentiment
that you have to do it for yourself, you don't need to prove
anything to anyone.

* * *

The first time I experienced Under Armour was in 2007 during
a tennis practice where my tennis shirt was soaking wet after
practice. My tennis coach, who also graduated from UMD

around the same time as Kevin Plank, told me about the UA sweat-wicking shirts. I went to buy one right after practice ended and immediately fell in love with the product. I have since studied the growth of the company from its first year of business in 1996 where it made $17,000 in sales out of Plank's grandmother's townhouse on the corner of 35th and O Street in Georgetown until now.

Just like Phil Knight believed so much in his idea by changing the way running shoes were designed, Kevin Plank believed that sweat-wicking shirts would change the way athletes not only performed but got dressed on the field. Kevin Plank noticed how it was so heavy to run in a sweat-soaked cotton shirt during football games, but also that the spandex shorts the players wore during games never weighed more than when dry, even when they sweat an insane amount. That is when he came up with the idea to create sweat-wicking shirts from the same type of design as spandex shorts, but for shirts to wear during practice and games that would not weigh any more, and would allow athletes to perform at their peak and not get stopped by any outside factor aside from their own performance.

Fight not to win, but to avoid losing. A surefire losing strategy.

- PHIL KNIGHT, *SHOE DOG*

This is not a strategy that companies trying to get ahead in the sports industry should ever attempt to do. If Under Armour did this, it would have never surpassed Adidas and become #2 regarding sports apparel sales in the United States. You fight to win. Regardless of what you are doing, whether you are on the field, the turf, in the pool, in a classroom, in your office. Under Armour is well aware of that. According to a Business Insider article, when Under Armour was first starting out its business, their "Protect This House" campaign fired up their business. It was seen as a mix of an authentic grassroots campaign with a rather small marketing budget. Somehow, they made it work really well.

Under Armour knew they had to rely a lot on marketing when it came to making a name for themselves in the industry, or else they would not have been able to set themselves apart right off the bat with big name competitors like Adidas and Nike already well established in the exact same market.

* * *

Nike and Under Armour both want everybody who wears their products to feel as though they are an athlete - because everyone is an athlete. Something I found really interesting about both companies' marketing strategies is that they both rely a lot on the feel-good feeling that the consumer will get after watching their advertisements.

For instance, Nike's Magic Soccer Night advertisement, part of their "Just Do It" campaign, recreates a sense of magic around playing your favorite sport, but for an older audience. They are using the reenactment of a spontaneous soccer game with older people to get the older consumers to purchase their goods and products - the hidden message of the ad is that they feel young again when they are playing their favorite sport, or in their happy place - which is what sports tends to do for a wide audience. They are also extremely strategic in the way that they end the ad in a powerful way by changing their tagline up with "Still Doing It."

I remember watching it on repeat for so long after I discovered it while working on a marketing project my sophomore year. I genuinely think it was after watching that exact ad that I knew I wanted to pursue sports marketing in my future and help create that same feeling that I felt while watching that ad. It had some sense of magic around it, something disillusioned about the harsh realities of life, something that holds you together for that one minute you are watching it because in that moment, you feel like you can do anything you set your mind to.

With that ad, Nike is saying in another way than Bill Bowerman's famous statement, that anyone is an athlete.

Under Armour does the same thing but changed the way

marketing was done by trying to empower their consumers through inspirational ads. Under Armour was really strategic in how they went about marketing their brand throughout the Olympics. Having Michael Phelps as one of their athletes, they created one of the most goosebumps inducing ad campaigns - the "Rule Yourself" series, that was actually named the best ad of 2016 by Ad Week.

You know how the saying "a picture is worth a thousand words" goes?

Under Armour took that to a whole new level, where their ad is entirely silent, and they let Michael Phelps' actions and dedications speak for themselves in the ad. The ad shows Michael Phelps' raw emotions, the pain he went through training for the Olympics, the amount of physical exhaustion he put himself through, but the ending tag-line of the ad explains that it is all worth it because "It's what you do in the dark that puts you in the light."

Under Armour hasn't stopped there - they are reinventing themselves in the sports marketing industry, especially by changing the way campaigns are done to target women specifically and make them feel like they can do the same, if not more, as their male equivalents. This is why their "I Will What I Want" campaign was created.

TAKEAWAY: LET'S SPARK A REVOLUTION

- A couple days ago, Under Armour revealed their new line of recovery sleepwear. *Cool?* I wholeheartedly think so. *Why?* Tom Brady said so.
  - THAT's the power of sports marketing. Tom Brady partnered with Under Armour to create this line of TB12 recovery sleepwear, and with his seal of approval, everyone who is a Brady fan, a football fan, or an athlete will buy into it.
  - As every athlete knows, recovery is extremely important, but so is the individual *who* is endorsing the product.
- Nike and Under Armour found ways to revolutionize the sports marketing industry by leveraging every strength and weakness they found within millennials
  - Millennials are opinionated, they like to talk about issues. *Let's give them something to talk about.*
    - Nike gave them something to talk about by designing self lacing shoes inspired by Back to The Future.
    - Under Armour gave them something to talk about with their TB12 sleepwear recovery line.

PART 3

THE GREATEST SPORTS MARKETING CAMPAIGNS

CHAPTER 8

UNDER ARMOUR'S "I WILL WHAT I WANT" CAMPAIGN

After a couple years on the market, Under Armour wanted to reinvent itself.

They realized that they held an "uber masculine image" and that the reason their brand was not performing as strongly as they could was that women were not attracted to the company.

As a TIME article written in 2014 stated, "most consumers associate Under Armour with the tight-fitting shirts that wick away football players' sweat." Not only that but in case study conducted by Droga5, they found that athletic women - women who are more focused on fitness than extreme performance - outright rejected the brand.

Actually, they saw Under Armour as "meat headed," "aggressive," "purely performance driven," and "definitely not for me." Under Armour wanted to change that image and those perceptions of its brand. They wanted to find a way to acquire women consumers, while also empowering them to perform at their utmost capacities through an inspiring campaign.

Inspire me please.

As it is widely known, most women shop at Lululemon and Nike when it comes to purchasing their workout gear - regardless as to whether it is for their "athleisure" purposes or actually getting down and dirty when they workout.

Under Armour wanted to acquire some of that target market by launching their most expansive campaign to date, costing a total of $15 million. As described in Droga5's case study, the campaign that Under Armour was going to bring out could not be "the typical *you go girl* message, brought to her by a sports brand, telling her she can do it *just like the boys*. Under Armour needed a truth that would prove to her that, unlike any other brand, Under Armour understands her."

Understand me please.

Under Armour conducted their research with Droga5, their advertising agency, and looked up the cultural context of the women of today: a woman of struggle. A woman who is told one thing one day, and something completely different the next day - *thereby denying her the power to decide for herself.*

I Will What I Want.

The first "I Will What I Want" advertisement that was launched featured American Soloist for the American Ballet Theatre, Misty Copeland. What distinguished this ad from any other one is the fact that her rejection letter from when she was 13 years old and auditioned for a ballet academy was being read in the background. What made it incredibly powerful was that while the rejection letter was being read, Misty Copeland is shown performing while in Under Armour gear.

Discreet, yet very tasteful and inspiring.

Misty Copeland said, "I think every woman has her version of that rejection letter, like many women, I was told that I wasn't good enough and that I couldn't succeed, but I willed myself to where I am now. I think that's a message that resonates with all women. Success isn't handed to us: we earn it." *Amen. I have had my fair share of rejections in my time on this earth.*

I Will What I Want.

This incredibly powerful message set out to launch by Under

Armour was so successful it garnered 4 million views in just one week.

I Will What I Want.

This message stuck with me the first time I watched the Misty Copeland ad. She never gave up, even after she received such a harsh, and detailed rejection letter, telling her everything that was wrong with her, and nothing that was right.

It made me reevaluate everything in my life that I gave up on because someone told me that I couldn't do it.

What did they know?!

Under Armour's marketing is so effective because it made me not only want to prove people wrong, but it made me want to prove people wrong while wearing Under Armour gear, because *I Will What I Want.*

Cheesy? Maybe. Effective? 100%.

The "I Will What I Want" ad campaign did not end there. In fact, Under Armour wanted to create controversies around their ad campaign so that they could get to the center of a cultural conversation that was already going on, just never put into the spotlight.

Under Armour wanted to free the woman and allow her to define success for herself, to stop listening to what society has to say, to defy expectations, and to ignore the noise about side judgments - *will beats noise.*

Let us defy expectations - I am tired of just sitting on the sidelines. Put me in coach.

That is why Under Armour chose to sign a woman whom they knew would be judged - supermodel Gisele Bündchen. They knew people would inevitably have things to say, comments to write - and they were right. Two days after signing Gisele, Under Armour and Droga5 took all the comments people had about the signing and partnership, and used those comments in an ad with Gisele, further developing the "I Will What I Want" series.

Gisele Bündchen said, "Will what you want is creating what you want. It is not listening to the outside noise. It is manifesting what it is that you want in your life."

She may be a Victoria's secret model and married to Tom Brady, but speaking those words, Gisele is an athlete to me. It is true - no matter what a woman does, she should not listen to outside factors deterring her from doing her best.

Remember that one friend I told you about who asked me in a

condescending tone why I always sign up for half-marathons, or as she put it "these things?"

I knew I had two options when it came to dealing with that: (1) letting her comments affect me and stop doing what it is that makes me feel alive and chasing that rush I can't get anywhere else, or (2) going out and proving to myself that no matter what anyone else says, I can and will do these things because I will what I want, and as Gisele said, I want to manifest what it is that I want in *my* life.

Gisele's "I Will What I Want" ad won multiple awards: The Cyber Grand Prix at Cannes, two gold lions and four silvers as well. Not only that but the campaign made Under Armour a symbol of female athletic aspiration. It generated 1.5 billion media impressions, website traffic went up 42%, and sales went up 28%. It also helped Under Armour become what is now the second largest sports apparel brand in the US. All it took was for them to target women in such a successful way.

The "I Will What I Want" campaign has since expanded in a very large way, they have signed more big name athletes, that include Lindsay Vonn, gold medalist Olympic alpine ski racer, and Kelley O'Hara, gold medalist defender on U.S. women's soccer. Women genuinely feel empowered by the campaign because as their ads say, "It doesn't matter what others think. It's what you believe."

Under Armour wants everyone to know that women can do whatever they want to do. On their "I Will What I Want" page on their website they have a statement that reads: "It doesn't matter what others think. It's what you believe. We're not a campaign; not a season or snapshot. Our story isn't told through a press release or social post. It's dripping down our backs–each drop a declaration to prove that the space between woman and athlete is no space at all. We're UA Women. And we WILL what we want."

Under Armour reinvented sports marketing by not only targeting women in a way that made them want to create a silent revolution in the athletic industry by defying expectations, no longer listening to outside noise, and doing what they want.

They did so in the most tactful of ways - targeting what was culturally hurting women and getting to the root of the problem, and saying the solution is not to buy Under Armour gear, but to go out and do what they want to do on their own terms. That creates a positive image in women's minds. They want to go out and do what they want, but in Under Armour gear.

CHAPTER 9

NIKE'S "JUST DO IT" CAMPAIGN

———

I still didn't believe in the power of advertising. At all. A product, I thought, speaks for itself, or it doesn't. In the end, it's only quality that counts. I couldn't imagine that any ad campaign would ever prove me wrong or change my mind.

- PHIL KNIGHT, SHOE DOG

Nike's "Just Do It" campaign has been around for as long as I can remember. I can say I definitely grew up with it, hearing all the "Just Do It" jokes possible, seeing the ads everywhere - if anything, the campaign's tagline can even be seen as Nike's slogan too.

"Just Do It" was inspired by Nike trying to target a larger audience than the "hyper-athletes" they were targeting when they first started out. Nike realized that they could not just target the athletes at the top of the pyramid because the market was 150 times larger when it came to everyone and anyone that could be considered an athlete - anyone with a body is an athlete, as Bill Bowerman once said.

In a BrandInsider article, it was discussed that Nike wanted to target the growing rates of obesity and find a way to inspire more people to go out on a run or go out and workout. As the article said, "Nike at this point in time had an opportunity to become the protagonist of all that was great and uplifting about the experience of sports and fitness."

With the help of Wieden+Kennedy, Nike came up with the "Just Do It" campaign. Three easy words, catchy, and somehow inspiring enough to get people off their couches. However, what really got this campaign to become an iconic symbol in the sports marketing world is *how* Nike actually advertises it.

Nike found inspiring ads that got people to *want* to go out on a run, or change their lifestyle habits for the better. In a way, it is telling everyone to stop procrastinating what they wanted to do.

It has a much larger message than sports in general, and that is why it is so successful. If you want to start out that business, go out and just do it. If you want to go hike the tallest summit in the world, just do it. If you want to ace that test, just do it. The only thing is, you need to put in the hard work required to get the desired results.

Inspiring? Yes. Effective? 100%.

When I was in fifth grade, a guy in my class came in wearing a Nike t-shirt that said, "Make your good better, and your better best." I was really chubby growing up. I never had an issue with it until people started making fun of me. I went home one day crying about my weight and my mom told me to repeat what was on my classmates' shirt a few weeks earlier.

Make your good better, and your better best. What does this have to do with people making fun of my weight, Mom?

She wiped away my tears, and told me to go out there and prove everyone wrong. As a fifth grader, I still had no idea what that meant, but that summer I put all of my efforts into getting better at tennis and swimming. Not only did my performance improve radically, but the weight came off. *Just Do It.*

Nike's "Just Do It" campaign indirectly changed my life for the better, and it most definitely did for so many other people out there.

When you come out with an absolutely incredible campaign like Nike's "Just Do It," strategically, you have to develop it as far as you can. That is the only way to not only retain the loyal customers, but also acquire new ones, whether it be through inspirational ads that they saw from your campaign, or the strongest form of marketing: word of mouth.

Word travels fast and Nike's three words, "Just Do It" come up in a conversation that people hold on a daily basis because it is so motivational.

I put out a survey to ask my friends what they thought of when they thought of sports marketing. When I asked the question: "When you think of sports marketing, do you think of a specific brand?" 87.5% of respondents said yes. When I asked which brand they thought of, 67% of respondents answered with "Nike." Going off of that question, I asked what campaign of that brand they thought of and 50% said "Just Do It." When I asked if they purchased that brand's products, 100% of respondents said yes.

That is there to show just how incredibly powerful Nike's campaign is - 100% of the respondents bought Nike gear. Nike mastered the formula to have so many people hooked in thinking if you wear the brand, you can "Just Do It."

Nike's "Just Do It" campaign is still relevant to date, so many people love it. In chapter 7, I showed how incredible Nike's "Magic Soccer Night" ad was. It is part of the "Just Do It campaign," only modified to say, "Still Doing It."

Nike's message goes beyond - never stop doing what you love.

Nike revolutionized the sports marketing industry, and is still a dominant player with their continuous ads and the continuous recognition consumers associate with not only the tagline, but the swoosh as well.

* * *

Growing up, sports was always present in my life. It was my safety net, my comfort zone, my escape, my outlet, my happy place. I think the reason that I love sports as much as I do is because it was the only way I saw that I made my dad proud.

My dad is my hero; the person I want to be. He loves sports and can spit out any facts about his favorite teams. When I was growing up, I didn't have much in common besides sports with him. I always wanted to impress him, so I used to try extra hard to win my swim meet or tennis match. He was always so proud of me in those moments. I cherished those moments because I didn't see him show how proud he was of me otherwise. Deep down, somewhere, I knew he was no matter what, but he never showed it apart from my athletic accomplishments.

I guess what is incredible about sports in general, and why I still want to be a part of that world going into my career, is that no matter what is going on in the world, for just a while, sports makes everyone come together. We are united as one. Win or lose, we are all one community, one family, rooting for our team, sharing in their victory, or their loss.

Go after it.

I've always been really good at running away from things. I don't like facing my emotions - I am a millennial after all... Actually, that is why I *used* to love running. It was my comfort zone. It was my safe place, my happy place. However, writing this book, I learned that as I get older, I cannot keep running away from things.

If Phil Knight or Kevin Plank ran away when things got hard, no one would be walking around wearing Flyknit sneakers or going to bed wearing TB12 sleepwear recovery.

Over the course of the last six or seven months that I have been writing and re-writing this book, I have changed a lot. I realized that I no longer want to *wait* for my confidence to magically show up. As a woman playing sports, I grew up being put down or always put on the bench or sidelines to watch.

You cannot do anything by just sitting watching on the

sidelines. In a sense, I felt like I was sitting on a bench or standing in the sidelines, watching my life unfold itself in front of me, play by play, without running onto the field and choosing to build my confidence.

I *choose* to believe in me.

I *choose* to believe that as a woman, I can break into the sports marketing industry and make a difference.

I *choose* to believe that following my passion will be rewarding and I am willing to wait.

I *choose* to dive into that pool full of unknowns and uncertainties.

I have to face things head on, I have to take risks, I have to be willing to fall, and I have to be willing to test out where my safety net is. I also found a new meaning to why I love running.

Bonnie Pfeister describes why I love running really accurately when she says, "I don't run because I love the feeling of running, I run because it makes me love the feeling of living."

I love running because it gives me life. It makes the good days better, and the bad days, good ones. I also learned that I have to trust myself in knowing that things will work out, I just cannot plan every aspect of my day. If you think about it, sports marketing has changed to target people like me.

Sports marketing looks to target people through their emotions and make them confident in their decisions. It looks to speak to us, millennials, past the physical aspect of our sports or workouts, but to speak to us by targeting our current emotional states and finding a way to be that safety net we all believe we need. Targeting us by being there for us when nothing else is.

Targeting the millennial, exactly like me.

Sports marketing has seen that millennials always have things weighing on their shoulders. That is really effective. Their ads have made me confident that brands like Nike, Adidas, and Under Armour will be there for me when I don't only need that supportive sports bra, but also need that supportive friend that is shown through their ads – the version of me who is stronger after that one workout because anything is possible.

Sports marketing has changed to adapt to the different set of problems its consumer is facing. Sports marketing found a way to be that shoulder the consumer wants to lean on when all else fails. Coca Cola does so in its ads that promote happiness.

By writing this book, I am aware that I am doing something out of my comfort zone – I am willingly putting my passion and myself out there for everyone to judge, for everyone to make or form their own opinion. The thing is, as the process of writing this book went on, I changed my outlook on it. Sports and sports marketing is what I love and what I am passionate about, so if that means someone out there is judging me on my passions, I did something right because it triggered something in them for them to react to.

So, this is me, putting myself out there for someone to judge, for someone to have an opinion, for someone to look up to, and for someone to say something about what I wrote. That is exactly what sports marketing is. Sports marketing is a brand putting itself out there, for the world to see, for the world to criticize, for the world to admire, and for the world to form their own opinions. My brand is me, and just like what is at the heart of sports marketing, sports is part of my brand.

Finding your passion is one thing, following it is another.

Everyone has something they are passionate about. Finding your passion may not be as hard as you think it is. The prob-lem is that not everyone goes after their passion. I can relate, it is scary to dive your head and heart right into a pool with an unknown depth or outcome.

What if I can't swim? You won't know unless you try. Tread water if you have to.

I genuinely believe that putting yourself out there and taking a risk, you will have known that at the very least, *you tried.*

Trying is the first step.

When I first came to Georgetown, everyone kept quoting Confucius by saying, "choose a job you love, and you will never have to work a day in your life." Somehow, as time went on, this quote seemed to escape most people's minds during the internship and job search. That is why I chose to write this book. I chose to write it for so many reasons, and more reasons keep coming to me every day. I wanted people to remember that there is more to life than making money. There is more to this book than simply how fascinating and revolutionary sports marketing is, how it has evolved, or how millennials have shaped it. I want people to find what they are passionate about, face their fears, take a risk, find happiness by chasing after what their heart desires, stop choosing the conventional route.

Go and just do it, because you will what you want.

ACKNOWLEDGEMENTS

—

First and foremost, I want to thank my parents for always supporting me and being there for me. Thank you for always believing in me. Thank you for letting me follow my dreams. I would not be the person that I am today without you guys.

Dad - Thank you for making me go to swim and tennis practice, even when I was sick, because it made me the dedicated person I am today.

Mom - Thank you for driving me to practice and above all, for never missing a game, match, swim meet, regatta, and half marathon.

I want to thank my sister, Noora, for being herself. If it weren't for your confidence in yourself and belief in your dreams, I wouldn't be out here chasing mine. I love you little one.

I want to thank my best friend, Maria Bianculli, for always being there for me. Thank you for coming to all my races with the biggest of smiles. Thank you for picking me up when I am down and for just getting me. No one gets me like you do. Whether I am abroad or not, I know you will be the first person I want to tell everything to. Thank you for having stuck by me after having seen me scream like a dad at soccer games.

I also want to thank Eric Koester for encouraging me to write a book about my passion. This book would not have been possible without him. Thank you for seeing potential in me and for motivating me to go after something I never thought attainable.

Finally, I want to thank everyone who motivated me to push myself. All your doubts and "no's" brought me to where I am today. Thank you for saying, "but you won't make it as a woman in that industry," because I want to make sure that I damn well make it as a woman. Thank you for the push I needed to go out and break every barrier.

Either write something worth reading or do something worth writing about.

- BENJAMIN FRANKLIN

Made in the USA
Columbia, SC
22 June 2018